Appalachian Tales
& Heartland Adventures

Appalachian Tales
& Heartland Adventures

by Bill Landry

Celtic Cat Publishing   Knoxville

© 2011 Bill Landry

All rights reserved. No part of this publication may be reproduced, stored in a retrieval system, or transmitted in any form or by any means—electronic, mechanical, photocopy, recording, or other, except for brief quotations in written reviews, without the prior written permission of the publisher.

Celtic Cat Publishing
2654 Wild Fern Lane,
Knoxville, Tennessee 37931
www.celticcatpublishing.com

We look forward to hearing from you.
Please send comments about this book
to the publisher at the address above.

Manufactured in the United States of America
Frontispiece: Steve Moore
Book and cover design: Dariel Mayer

Publisher's Cataloging-in-Publication Data
Landry, Bill.
Appalachian tales & heartland adventures : a collection of stories, tales, and adventures from 25 years of the most successful local TV show in the region's history / by Bill Landry.
p. cm.
ISBN: 978-0-9819238-8-8 (hardcover)
ISBN: 978-0-9819238-7-1 (pbk.)
1. Tennessee—Social life and customs. 2. Appalachian Region—Social life and customs. 3. Heartland series (Television program). I. Title.
F440 .L36 2011
976.8—dc22   2011928033

For Becky

CONTENTS

Meet the Heartland Guy   ix

CHAPTER 1
The Story Begins   1

CHAPTER 2
Feeling Our Way   7

CHAPTER 3
Bear Tales   15

CHAPTER 4
Adventures on LeConte   25

CHAPTER 5
Nature's Guides and Unlikely Explorers   37

CHAPTER 6
April Fools   47

CHAPTER 7
Native Americans   57

CHAPTER 8
The Grips   69

CHAPTER 9
The Wit and Wisdom of the People 77

— COLOR PLATES —

CHAPTER 10
Stories, Tales, and Storytellers 93

CHAPTER 11
Moonshine Stories and Halloween Tales 107

CHAPTER 12
World War II Tales 117

CHAPTER 13
Real People 123

CHAPTER 14
Out of the Ordinary 131

CHAPTER 15
The Legend of Jonathan Swift's Lost Silver Mine 141

CHAPTER 16
Where Story Ideas Come From 151

CHAPTER 17
A Gathering of Friends 161

CHAPTER 18
The Epilogue 173

ACKNOWLEDGMENTS 177

CREDITS 179

INDEX 181

Meet the Heartland Guy

Sometimes it's weird being me. People come up to me on the street and say, "Hey, I know you . . . say something." Or, at a restaurant, they stare a bit before asking, "Hey! Do you know who you are?" and I reply, "Yeah, sometimes I do."

It took a while to get used to, but I remember Margie Ison, the Channel 10 weather person and East Tennessee icon, saying, "Be nice to all those people. They're the people you work for. They pay your salary." Today, I like it when people say, "Hey, there's the *Heartland* dude!" It means they watch the show and like our work. That's good. There's nothing wrong with that. In fact, it's very special.

I didn't set out in life to become the host and narrator of *The Heartland Series*. I played basketball and football and was captain of my teams at Notre Dame High School in Chattanooga. I went to the University of Chattanooga (now UTC) on a football scholarship and played for two years. Our all-America quarterback talked me into auditioning for Dorothy Hackett Ward's Shakespeare production. I got cast in the play, and was in every one after that.

I liked the theater and attended Dallas Theater Center in Texas on a scholarship to work on a Master of Fine Arts degree. I wrote my master's thesis while producing a bicentennial play titled "The History of Roane County, Tennessee." It had a cast of more than ninety folks, many of whom had never seen a live play before.

So the die was cast. I wrote, produced, and performed a one-man play about Albert Einstein called *Einstein the Man*. From 1977 through 1981, I traveled thirty-eight states and two provinces in Canada. Amazingly, I still travel to do that play and have performed it over a thousand times.

From 1982–1984, I worked for the Tennessee Valley Authority, first at the World's Fair Exhibit and then to celebrate TVA's Fiftieth Anniversary, aboard the Valley Adventure on the Tennessee River. As the "live" fake riverboat captain, my job involved hosting, presenting, and performing. This entailed lots of media work: television, promotions, and meeting thousands of valley residents. It was great training for my Channel 10 work on *The Heartland Series,* though I didn't know it then.

In 1984, I met Rod Kirby during a freelance commercial job for State Technical Institute (now, Pellissippi State Community College.) He worked at Channel 10 and suggested I talk to his boss, Steve Dean, about working at Channel 10. The rest is history, or should I say, the history of this book.

Today, my wife Becky and I live as quietly as we can in a log cabin that we built in 2007 in Blount County, Tennessee, next to the Great Smoky Mountains National Park. My son Jack, who is teaching theater in Wilmington, North Carolina, and who lands an occasional film role, and his wonderful wife Weatherly have our first grandchild, Hawk Augustus. Becky's boys, Michael and Ryan, are living in Oregon pursuing their careers and doing well. Whenever possible, they all come home to the mountains to visit.

I know I'm a very lucky man, with a loving family and so many good friends. I like to fish, write, talk, and direct, and I am happier than I've any right to be.

I'm fortunate indeed to be able to share these bits of Appalachian wisdom with you to use on your life's journey.

Bill Landry
Summer 2011

TVA Exhibit at the 1982 World's Fair in Knoxville, Tennessee.

Appalachian Tales
& Heartland Adventures

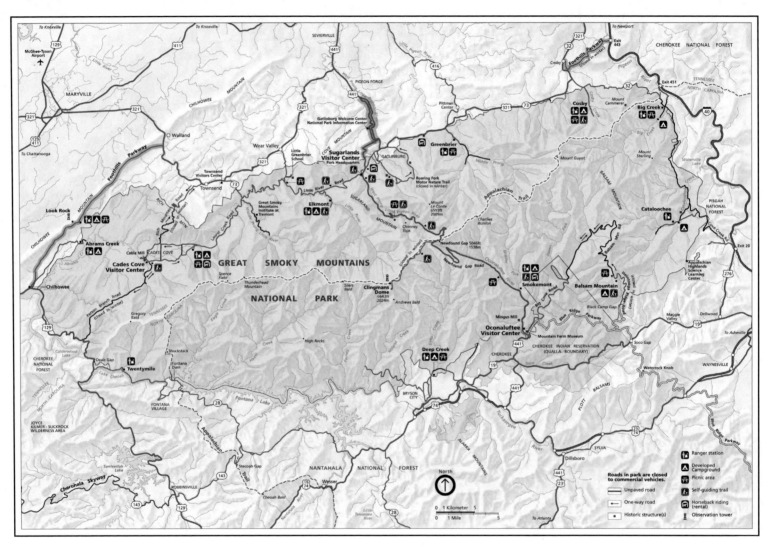

Regional map identifying the Great Smoky Mountains National Park.

CHAPTER I

The Story Begins

Since the decision was made in 2009 to stop production of *The Heartland Series,* the question I'm asked most often is, "Why did it end?" Prior to that time, the question asked most frequently was, "How did it all begin?"

This book attempts to describe a fascinating journey that began in 1984 and, over twenty-five years, resulted in the creation of more than nineteen hundred episodes. During those years, I was blessed to work on the show as host/narrator and co-producer, along with other talented friends and colleagues.

I wish I could remember all the stories that made the exploration so enjoyable. Within these pages are some of my favorites. Some I heard; others actually happened and are recorded for the first time. By presenting them here, hopefully, you will better understand, enjoy, and experience these adventures, travels, and stories. More importantly, this book will enable us to remember those good people who first told these tales, and preserve the history of how they lived.

The Vision

It was two years after the 1982 World's Fair in Knoxville, but the region still was buzzing from successfully hosting a party for the world. There was a new confidence and energy in the air.

Channel 10 recognized this. It was a business leader. For the previous decade, Channel 10 News had been the consistent ratings leader, with almost fifty percent of the region's viewers tuned to the station. No station in America had a higher percentage of viewers.

The station wanted to do something to celebrate the fiftieth anniversary of the founding of the Great Smoky Mountains National Park. Steve Dean, the Creative and Community Services Director and his boss, General Manager Jim Hart, developed the vision for *The Heartland Series* and named it after the station's logo, "Straight from the Heart."

Jim Hart was an avid hiker and supporter of the National Park. He wanted the *Series* to capture and showcase the beauty and magnificence of the mountains. Steve Dean, the Executive Producer, made it happen. The idea was to take the camera out of the studio, record the majestic views provided by the Park, and interview the mountain people while they were still alive and able.

Initially, Steve wanted to shoot the entire series on high-end film and then transfer it to video. This proved too costly an option, so we settled on us-

Old postcard advertising trout fishing.

ing a very expensive Ikigami camera to produce exceptional video pictures.

I was hired on a three-month contract in March 1984 to work on two pilot episodes: "William Bartram—The Flower Hunter," and "Lucinda," the story of Lucinda Oakely Ogle. By June, Union Carbide became the first sponsor of the *Series* and my contract was extended for a year.

Jack Harper, Public Relations Director of Union Carbide, liked the idea of introducing his company's new management team at the Department of Energy facilities in Oak Ridge. He took the pilot programs to Ken Jarmalo, the CEO of Union Carbide operations in Oak Ridge, and they sponsored the initial year.

We were committed to producing two episodes a week through 1984 and they would alternate in four different time slots: at 6:55 a.m., after the morning news; at 12:25 p.m., after the noon news; at 5:55 p.m., before the nightly news; and finally at 11:25 p.m.

Rod Kirby was the camera man/videographer. Doug Mills was soundman and Rod's assistant. Sean Kirk and Laura Armour were writer/producers. I was the host and narrator. Steve Dean, with help from Joe Cable, edited almost all of the stories in our first year.

The first story was scheduled to air in July 1984. For as long as we worked on the *Series,* we were always trying to get ahead. This meant having stories shot and "in the can." The only stories we had in the can were the two pilot programs and two stories with Dr. Stuart Maher about the ancestral mountains and the coves. That gave us four shows.

In the twenty-five years of *The Heartland Series,* we probably never had any more shows in the can than that. We just could never get ahead. It was like the myth of Sisyphus, that poor guy that gets up every day and pushes the rock up the hill only to have it roll back down. Then, the next day he gets up and starts pushing that rock again. That was always us.

The First Heartland Story: The Bohanons

Videographer Doug Mills reminded me recently that this was the start of two grueling days. We had to shoot "wraps," which means me on camera at the Little Greenbrier Schoolhouse for the story with Elsie Burrell. Later, we were meeting Kim Delozier and shooting a story on the European wild boar. Then early the next day, we had to head up Kirkland Falls for a brook trout story.

We began by heading to the "Y" in Townsend, Tennessee, to get some footage of fly fishermen for the brook trout story. Originally, all the streams in the Park were populated with these native trout, the Appalachian Brook Trout.

We arrived at the Little River above Townsend. We had exactly an hour before we needed to head to Greenbrier. Doug was shooting and John Davis was helping him, gripping and doing sound. We had time to shoot some B-roll—that's what TV people call extra pictures/shots to be used and edited into the story. We were above Townsend where the east fork of Little River, which comes from Cades Cove, and the west fork from Elkmont, join together with the middle prong of the Little River from Tremont.

There were two old guys fishing. We could see them from the bridge. They kept catching trout, one after another. It was pretty cool. They didn't look like fishermen. They looked like mountain men. And that's exactly what they were.

One was tall and lanky. He wore hip boots. He didn't have on full body waders that fancy trout fishermen wear. Not this tall drink of water. He was a lean mountain man and wore old school black hip boots that tied to his belt.

The other guy, his brother, was a little heavier and shorter. He fished with two little split shots for weights. He used nymphs and wet flies that sunk the fly down near the bottom of the river, because they always told me that's where the trout are!

The tall guy used, and this is unbelievable, twelve-pound monofilament fishing line on his fly reel! He had it tied to a little leader, then to two flies separated by a split shot. The flies looked like doodlebugs or big gobs of knitting wool with a little thread around them. Because that's about

Walter and A.D. Bohanon trout fishing.

what they were: big gobs of wool tied to a huge number 4 or 6 size hook. Boy, did they catch trout.

I introduced myself to Walter Bohanon first. He was nearest to the bank, and I asked him if we could talk.

"Sure," Walter replied in a friendly sort of way.

But as he began sliding over through the stream to where we were, I could see he was a bit unsure of what I was doing. I told Walter we were from WBIR and doing a short TV show on trout fishing. I asked him if we could talk to him a little.

"I reckon," Walter said.

Doug had the camera positioned and John Davis was trying to get a handle on using Rod's

"This book will enable us to remember those good people who first told these tales, and preserve the history of how they lived."

Walter Bohanon shows me how to tie trout flies.

reflector. Rod Kirby had made it by covering a piece of cork board with aluminum foil to reflect light. John was holding it, trying to put some light on Walter and me. I explained to Walter what we were doing. "We're trying to learn about brook trout. Would you mind helping us by talking in full sentences for the TV? Sound bites, you know."

"Sure," he said.

"So, Sir . . . Walter, can you give me your full name?"

"Sure," he said. Then there was a long pause.

I looked at Doug. Doug looked at me. We both looked at Walter and he smiled. Then I said something like, "Hey Walter, we need you to talk in full sentences so we can use it on TV. You know, as we talk about living in the Smoky Mountains." Walter nodded. He understood perfectly, way better than I did. I'd only been doing this interview thing for about a month myself.

Doug motioned to me that the camera was on. I said, "Okay, Mr. Bohanon. Where did you grow up?"

Walter said, "Big Greenbrier."

"Hold it, Doug, just a minute. No, Walter, can you say it in a complete sentence, like, 'I grew up in Big Greenbrier.' "

[4]   Appalachian Tales & Heartland Adventures

"Yep," he said.

It went on like Abbot and Costello for about ten more minutes. Then, his brother, A.D. came over. That's when *The Heartland Series* was born.

Like he was befriending us, A.D. proceeded to tell us what it was like to grow up in the Great Smoky Mountains. He said, "Tell those park rangers, if they want some of these brook trout, tell 'em to go away up in the high mountains and catch some. These trout they got down here, they ain't brook trout. They're the rainbow. They got them big heads. Those brook trout got them little bitty heads. These trout down here they're all mixed up! They're not the native trout. Now my brother, he's been here fishing for 'bout sixty-nine years. I reckon he's been here long enough to be called one of the natives! Ha! Now, we don't want to argue with no one. Trout's trout! We like to fish."

When viewed back in the studio, this video looked just like a Norman Rockwell painting. We showed Steve the interview with A.D. and Walter Bohanon, thinking we'd done well with this B-roll footage as background for the brook trout story. Steve got real excited and completely forgot about the brook trout story for the time being.

"Here's the show," he said. "Listen to what they're saying. They're telling you what it was like to grow up in the Great Smoky Mountains! They're as good as any man and they know it. Listen to how they talk, like they're sons of these mountains, and they know them."

It wasn't so much what they said, but how they said it that Steve was talking about. Quickly, Steve wrote a little introduction for me to say, and we began putting together the story and called it "Fishin'." It began with me saying something like, "I'd like you to meet two new friends of ours, A.D. and Walter Bohanon, streamside philosophers."

And then, we simply aired the interview and let A.D. talk. We didn't interrupt him or overwrite the story. This is important: WE LET HIM TELL HIS OWN STORY. Steve always said that was when *The Heartland Series* was born. We learned to let the people tell their own story.

We only had about eighteen minutes of tape of the Bohanons, one raw video tape. But it was enough. We had a few shots of them fishing in Little River and a wide shot of them standing there. That was it. Steve and Joe edited the story and made it work.

For years afterwards, every Christmas, at least until they died, we tried to see A.D. and Walter. We did other stories with them, too. Walter tied flies, great trout fishing flies. He kept me stocked with them for years. I went trout fishing with them many times. They probably taught me more about how to trout fish than anyone.

A.D. cut a Christmas tree with his grandson one year while we taped it for a Christmas story. We always tried to keep in touch with them and their huge family. For years, even after they died, we'd meet another Bohanon somewhere or other. Still do. There must be millions of them for A.D. and Walter had about six or eight other brothers and sisters.

A Heartland Christmas at the Mountain View Hotel

At the end of the year, we had the first and only Heartland Christmas Party. It was held in Gatlinburg at the Mountain View Hotel. It was a celebration of the *Series,* Christmas, and the coming together of all our friends. We invited everyone who appeared in the episodes that first year, our sponsors, and all the Channel 10 support people. It

"Here's the show. Listen to what they're saying . . . listen to how they talk, like they're sons of these mountains, and they know them."
—Steve Dean

1928 picture of the Mountain View Hotel, Gatlinburg, Tennessee.

was very similar to our last "Gathering of Friends," held twenty-five years later at the Museum of Appalachia in August 2009.

To see the "suits" from the corporate world laughing and talking with A.D. and Walter Bohanon, along with the Shape Note Singers, and quilters, Lucinda, Dr. Sharp, and everyone else was priceless.

Walter Bohanon was so taken with Union Carbide's President, Ken Jarmalo, he gave him a big twist of his "bull-faced" chewing tobacco. Mr. Jarmalo took a big "chaw" too. Being neighborly, I guess. Jim Hart ran over, trying to stop him from taking it. "No, no, don't take that!" But it was too late.

It wasn't that Jim had anything against Walter's friendly gift or expression of kindness. On the contrary, he just knew the power and potential strength of bull-faced chewing tobacco, particularly the stout kind that Walter made. It put hair on billiard balls. We heard later that Mr. Hart was forced to stop for water more than once on the way home to put out the fire in Ken Jarmalo's mouth.

It wasn't long after the party that they closed the historic Mountain View Hotel and sold it. They leveled the land and turned it into an amusement park, but that little Christmas party was a night to remember.

CHAPTER 2

Feeling Our Way

Post-Production Magic

It has been more than twenty-five years since we started the *Series*. Often, I've wondered what would've happened had we not found our first sponsor, or our fiftieth. It was a constant marketing struggle to support the project. Sales Manager Lynn Leopper and Jim Hart's efforts got it started and kept it going.

I went to work for Channel 10 on that short-term contract. I was hired to do two pilot episodes. If they sold, I would have a job for a year, maybe two. I stayed for twenty-five years. Wow! Life really is what happens while you're busy making other plans.

People ask me if I thought the show would be as successful as it was and whether I thought it would last that long. My answers are, "Yes, I thought it would be very successful," and "No, not really. I didn't know it would last for twenty-five years!"

When we finished shooting "William Bartram" and came in to the studio to work on post-production, I was amazed. That's when I found out what magic Steve Dean could do to make the stories sing—through putting music and shots together, dissolves, fades to black, all the techniques of good editing, and great post-production television work.

Steve was great with music too. He hired Tom Jester, Michael Ginsburg, Evan Carawan, and Cathy Leach to develop our *Heartland* theme music. The music came from an old Scottish ballad/tune called "Heman Dubh" which means "black rock." Another tune we used was an old Irish ballad, a wonderful melody called, "The Minstrel Boy to War Has Gone." I can hear it now in my head. It's so distinctive. That first year we also used the theme from *Jeremiah Johnson*, Copland's *Appalachian Spring*, and Dvorak's *New World Symphony*. With these choices, viewers began to see our people and these majestic mountains with a new heroic coloring. Such was the effect of classical music; it dignified and elevated our perception of ourselves.

It was in post-production that Steve, Joe, Ken McWhirter, and all our editors continued to work on the three-minute-and-forty-second features until each show produced an enormous amount of emotion. Fade in, fade out. Go to black. I had no idea such beauty and magic could be created. I knew a little bit about what I was doing, but I had no idea what Steve Dean, Joe Cable, and Doug Mills were doing, or Linda Billman, Sean Kirk,

Lynn Leopper, Sales Manager, WBIR.

Joe Cable, Writer/Producer/Editor, WBIR.

Mary Katherine (Alexis) Magnotti, Amy Palmer, Ernie Ingle, Laura Armour, and others who contributed. We were all involved and working on it together. Steve directed us so that we could collectively produce and create a wonderful little story. Of course, we were working seven days a week and that had a lot to do with the quality of the product.

That first year was a blur. We didn't know how to do much of anything. No one had ever done it before. We just did it by trial and error. Looking back on it now, twenty-five years later, I realize we did it the hard way!

We did fifty-two episodes in six months. That's two episodes a week—every week. Plus, we did two excellent half-hour shows that first year. One of them, "Paradise Recaptured," won a lot of awards. We usually didn't finish editing the first episode until Thursday or Friday night. Then, we'd start editing the second episode, often rewrite it, tweak it, and finish it sometimes as late as 6:00 p.m. on Sunday. We'd go home, have dinner with our families, and Monday morning we'd start again. This went on for years! The second and third years, we did ninety-six and ninety-four episodes respectively. We did thirty-minute specials every year as well. That was a lot of work. But we loved it.

Paradise Recaptured— When Sean Ate Carpet

The first half-hour special was "Paradise Recaptured," which told the story of the establishment and preservation of the nation's most visited national park, the Great Smoky Mountains National Park. Sean Kirk, our first writer/producer, worked himself silly. He'd been up for days pulling all-nighters, along with all the rest of us. For non-TV folks, that's simply working all night long without sleep and doing it for days. It's not very healthy, to say the least. Sean hadn't eaten much either.

We were nearing the crucial point in editing where the show was being mixed on the fly, as they say. That's after all the shots are in the master, and natural sound is added—like the sound of streams or birds singing. Music also is added. Normally, this doesn't happen while the actual show is being run on TV. However, in this instance, we didn't have enough time to mix the show. So, we were adding the sound and music as it was actually airing! That's scary and crazy. You don't want to do that because too many things can go wrong. If you make a mistake, you can't fix it. It's ON THE AIR!

This was extremely nerve-wracking. It was our first time doing a special at the end of our first year, and we didn't know any other way to do it. As the final master of "Paradise Recaptured" was being mixed ON THE AIR, Sean Kirk jumped up in the master control room and flipped out! He flopped around on the ground like a fish, and ate carpet. That's the TV slang for it.

He passed out and went into convulsions. We thought he was going to die. But we couldn't stop the mix because it was on the air. There wasn't anything to do but move him over, let him flop around on the side, and continue to mix the show. Sean was promptly carried out on a stretcher by men in white coats. I didn't see it myself, because I was in another room watching the show. The next day we went to see him at the hospital and he appeared to be fine, as fine as Sean Kirk could ever be. His body just freaked out. It reacted poorly to days and nights of no food and sleep.

It was a good lesson learned. Do not try to do this at home! You don't ever want to work so hard you don't eat or sleep for days. If you do, you'll eat carpet, like Sean. That became the warning cry at Channel 10.

One other Sean Kirk story has to do with the Christmas story he wrote that first year. It was called "A Gift for Jacob," and won the prestigious New York International Film and TV Festival award. Sean went home to New Jersey to show his mother the work he'd been doing. For some reason, most of our families had no idea what our work was in those days. Maybe most of them were just glad we were working and didn't care!

That first year, we all made copies of some of our favorite *Heartland* episodes, the ones we were proudest of, and brought them home for Christmas. We wanted to make our families proud. We couldn't wait to hear how Sean's mother expressed her pride in Sean for writing a piece that won a medal. "Oh, she said she liked it a lot, but she kept asking me, 'What's a Fried Pie?' " Of course he said this with a thick, exaggerated, New Jersey accent. Then he giggled like always. I don't think they eat a lot of fried pies in New Jersey!

A similar thing happened to me the third year when I went home to Chattanooga. I brought some of the first VHS *Heartland* tapes to show my family. Like Sean's mother, my father didn't react the way I thought he might. In those early *Heartland* episodes we'd not yet removed those "wraps," where I introduce the stories and the title of the show before and after each episode.

They all had something like, "Hi, I'm Bill Landry and today we're going to climb LeConte." Then, three minutes later, I'm back on camera saying, "This is still *The Heartland Series,* and I'm still Bill Landry!" My family gathered for Christmas in the TV room to watch "Billy's TV show." When the tape started, there was a hush. They watched a couple of shows. Then my father started getting antsy. He'd call it fidgety. He'd sit up. Then, he'd turn and look over at me. He'd look back at the TV for a while. Finally, after the third or fourth episode, he jumped up and blurted out "Jeez! We know who you are!"

Sean and I had a pretty good laugh about that. Our families can always keep us in our place. They never miss an opportunity to remind us who we are, or where we came from.

Start of VHS and DVD Sales

It was serendipity that got us into selling tapes and DVDs. It started out as a way to provide a service to those people who shared their lives with us. We had a VHS recording machine in the *Heartland* office and made copies of the stories they were

Heartland crew, 1985. Laura Armour, Doug Mills, Sean Kirk, and yours truly in Oak Ridge. Note the "subject to search" sign.

Steve Dean, *Heartland* **Executive Producer.**

Jim Hart, General Manager, WBIR.

Ranger Kim Delozier with recently trapped wild hog.

featured in. Without those folks, our subjects, we wouldn't have squat.

Later, when we received enough requests for both single episodes and the entire first year of the *Series,* Steve Dean and Jim Hart made the decision to start running off copies of the episodes to sell to the general public. This helped defray operating costs.

One problem was the lack of resources to help us do this. I remember spending Christmas after Christmas in the mail room at WBIR, putting boxes of tapes together. Man, we spent hours and hours in December boxing tapes, trying to get them out for Christmas. Everybody had to pitch in. We even brought our children in to help us—that's about the only way we could see them much before Christmas! I'm kidding, but only a little.

Mostly, we sold them at the front desk of the station but, around the same time, through Glenn Cardwell's efforts at the Great Smoky Mountains National Park, the National Park began to offer our tapes for sale to the general public at visitor centers.

Tales of the "Tourons"

There's a story about our shooting "wraps." They introduced or concluded the story. I would stand there, or walk and talk to the camera. We'd do this after spending all day climbing a mountain, or hiking twelve miles with a naturalist; each of us carrying forty pounds of lunch and TV gear. Whew! We also tried to have a "God shot" at the beginning and end of each episode, something with a spectacular view of the mountains.

We'd arrive and park at an overlook, and tourists would honk at us as they went by. People would shout at us, "Hey, TV! Put us on TV!" I would be off to one side trying to memorize my lines. The producer/writer, Sean or Laura, would be hollering new lines at me. "Hey, these are better lines!" The sun would be setting rapidly and Doug, conscious of the traffic, low batteries, and fading light, would be nervous as a chicken in a barnyard on Sunday. We had to get it right on the first take! We just didn't have any time, batteries, or sunlight left!

That's when a big white Cadillac might pull over and honk. It would pull up between the camera and me, right in the middle of our shot. Some guy would get out wearing black shoes and white socks. He'd have striped shorts, a polka-dotted shirt, and thick, black-rimmed glasses. Completely unaware he was interrupting anything at all, he'd say, "Hey! Is this the road to GATTLES-BUOIG?"

We all looked at each other and said, "Yeah! Go on down the mountain, straight ahead! You can't miss it! It's the only place this road leads to!"

Sean came up with the term for this strange breed of mammal that comes to this area in droves every year. "Tourons!" he called them. We had a lot of fun with them and even did entire episodes about them. We figured they were all from Ohio and every place north of here was Ohio!

Park Ranger, Kim Delozier, tells a lot of funny stories about tourists. He started working for the Park as a "hog hunter" about the same time we started the *Series*. We did dozens of wildlife stories with Kim over the years, including the red wolf reintroductions, elk introductions, even "elf" introductions. Over time, Kim became the head biologist in Wildlife Management for the National Park, and a great friend.

One day near Tremont, a lady came up to Kim and asked emphatically, "How many trees are there in the Smokies?"

"Pardon me, madam?" Kim said.

She insisted all the more. "How many trees you got? How many trees are there in the National Park? Don't you know?"

Once, a lady came up to him in Cades Cove and said, "Your fences are loose and your deer are out!"

"Ma'am," Kim said, "The deer can jump over those fences."

"I don't care," she said, "Your fences are broke and your deer are out!"

That's the kind of stuff tourons say. They don't know any better. They're not from here. They're usually from Ohio.

In Cataloochie, a guy once pointed to a thousand-pound wild elk and said to Kim, "Hey, Buddy. What's it cost to ride one of them?"

"You can't ride it," Kim said. "It's an elk!"

"But I'll give you ten dollars to ride that elk!"

Another time, Doug and I were driving around Cades Cove shooting video for a summer story. Just like all the rest of the tourists, we were caught in slow traffic on the Cades Cove loop road. Up ahead, we could see there was a "bear jam." Now, that's simply where a bear, usually a pretty big bear, is foraging near the road, often with her cubs. Tourons will jump out of their cars and run up to within six feet of the bear and take pictures. It can be fairly dangerous.

But just like the Tourons, that's often how we got some of our best bear footage. We just happened to be in the right place, at the right time. This day Doug was parked by the side of the road shooting video of a bear when a fellow walks up and says, "Whatcha doin'?"

Tourists getting too close to a young bear.

Cris Gallu, National Sales Manager, WBIR.

Now, he's being friendly. It's just that Doug Mills, a professional videographer, with a multi-thousand dollar camera and a thirty-pound tripod, is shooting video of a nearby Mama bear and her cubs.

"Watcha doin'?" is something Doug's heard about five thousand times. It didn't use to bother him—but somewhere along the way he snapped. Maybe it was around year eighteen or so. He started to reply, "Oh, I don't know . . . I'm eating," or "I'm going swimming."

Now in all fairness, what the touron actually wants to know is, "What's that video going to be used for?" So here we are on a sunny summer afternoon in Cades Cove. Doug's taking pictures of this nice Mama bear and her three cubs when the guy says, "Whatcha doin'!?"

I look at Doug and see him smiling a bit, but he doesn't move his head from the lens. Then the touron surprises us. "Hey, how did you know the bears would be out here today?"

Feeling a little mischievousness might be in order, I say, "Well, it's nearly two o'clock, isn't it?" And the big man from Ohio says, "Why yes . . . it is."

"Well, the rangers said they'd feed the bears at two o'clock. So, here we are. It's two o'clock!"

"Oh yeah, I see," he says.

Tourons are a strange and harmless species, unless you get behind them in traffic. Then, they're maddening.

Ethel Goes to Chicago

I began this chapter alluding to the need to find sponsors to keep the *Series* going. Television isn't about great art and drama. It's not about uplifting human experience and affairs. It's not about education or promoting cultural events and better understanding of our fellow man. It's about selling time. That's it.

Year after year, we had to find four corporations who were willing to put up large sums of money to pay for the right to sponsor the programming we were producing. It was a constant struggle.

One day Cris Gallu, the current National Sales Manager, came into our office and asked us to put together five or six of our best shows. He said he was going to Chicago to present them to big Execs. "The 'suits' will all be there; Coca Cola, Toyota, and the Ford Motor Company!" He slapped his hands together. "We'll show those boys from the big city about our people, how beautiful it is here. We'll get this thing sponsored!"

So we put together a short tape with Wiley Oakley's "The Cow Barn," and Maynard Ledbetter's "The Homeplace," featuring spectacular video from Cades Cove. We added a few other favorite stories, too, including Ethel Birchfield's story. Ethel, who dipped snuff, told old English riddles and lived in a little place on Roane Mountain up near Elizabethton, Tennessee, and Boone, North Carolina. Collectively, these early shows depicted the spectacular beauty of the mountains and the character and personality of the region and its people.

On Tuesday or Wednesday the following week, we saw Cris and asked him how it went, anticipating perhaps a big raise or, at least the continuation of our jobs for one more year. We were always involved in helping to find sponsors for the show, year after year.

Cris had on his freshly starched shirt and tie,

and clapped his hands together as he described his business trip to Chicago.

"Boys," he said, "they loved "The Cow Barn," and they loved Maynard Ledbetter's people, and they'd never seen anything in their lives as beautiful as Cades Cove. They loved the mountains and the streams and the people. When Ethel came on and started telling those riddles, hey, they liked that too when she was just sitting there. But when she spit off the front porch . . . Damn," he said, "Ethel killed us in Chicago!"

A Riddle

One more thing about Ethel. Her talent or gift for riddles was very unusual, even for the mountain people. She knew and could remember exactly old English riddles and ballads. The origins of the songs and riddles dated back hundreds of years. They certainly predated this country's short existence.

Apart from Ethel "killing us in Chicago," it took a pretty astute and eclectic mind to understand what Ethel was about. If you can't get by her chickens in the front yard and the fact she dipped a little snuff, you probably will never understand her ability to remember and relate her tales.

I found one in some old papers. They're puzzles. You're supposed to try to guess the answer, what the riddle means, what it's about. It goes like this:

> As I went around my wheely, whorley,
>   wicken wackum,
> I met old tom, tickum tackem.
> To run old bomb bickum backum
>   out of my wheely,
> Whorley, wickum wackum.

People of the mountains, circa 1903.

I'll give you a hint: the wheely, whorley, wicken wackum is a wheat field. It's about an old man who sees a bull in his wheat field and he called his dog to run the bull out of the wheat field.

This is not exactly one of Ethel's riddles. It came from Jeanette Martin's grandpaw. She wrote it down for me, because it's hard to remember the words. It's a play on words. It's a riddle!

"He Told It fer the Truth"

I've always loved the saying "he told it for the truth." Obviously, it refers to telling a story and the teller means for us to believe it's true. As to whether all of these stories are true or not, you'll just have to "take 'em or leave 'em," as my Daddy used to say. Most of them are true. If not, they ought to be!

Now, in my collecting and writing them, I might stretch the truth a bit in order to make a better tale. But that's okay—at least, according to Ray Hicks's definition of what constitutes a good story. Ray, I believe, is the greatest storyteller in the world. I once asked him, "What's the difference between a story and a lie?" Ray answered in that old mountain drawl of his, "A stawry, Bill, is always the truuuth. But it's a stawry. So, you can tell it any old way, and it's still the truuth, but it's a stawry. When you tell a lie, you gotta tell seven more to prop it up. Then you can't keep 'em apart!"

So, that's what I'm saying here. These aren't lies or fiction. They're stories, and I'm telling them for the truth.

Bear walking in tall grass.

CHAPTER 3

Bear Tales

Bears in Hibernation

First of all, bears don't actually hibernate in caves. That's what Dr. Mike Pelton taught us when we did our first black bear episode. They climb to the top of old growth trees and use their sharp claws to dig out cavities left by owls or pileated woodpeckers, or they find natural holes big enough to crawl into for winter. They're much safer high atop trees than anywhere on the ground.

Dr. Pelton started the black bear program at the University of Tennessee and the Great Smoky Mountains National Park. His students are some of the best-trained wildlife biologists and researchers in the world, working on all sorts of critters: Belize jaguars, red wolves, wild boar, you name it.

"It's true," he said to us one day on camera, as we bent over and looked at a pile of bear scat, "bears do shit in the woods!"

Our job was to follow his team and tell the story of bears in hibernation. We'd already radio-collared a big Mama bear and knew she was somewhere in this section of the National Park. All we had to do was find her, climb up a ninety-foot tree, and take some pictures.

The trouble was that bears don't live in condos on the side of Ski Mountain near Gatlinburg. They like deep forests, steep ridges, and remote country. That's why Pelton's researchers are so well trained. When black bears move through the Smoky Mountains, it's all downhill to them. They don't mind running straight up a mountain for miles. They're built for that.

If you're a student researcher following your subject bear with a tracking device, you get used to scrambling up ridges, going hungry, and thinking like the animal you're tracking. Television people don't think like that. We're looking for the easier, softer way.

Finally, after about three hard miles, we climbed one more knoll. Pelton's bunch dropped all their gear, threw a rope up a tree, pointed upwards ninety feet in the air, and said, "She's up there."

"Shooting" isn't a good word to use when describing what it is we do with the camera, particularly when referring to wildlife. But, it's what we do.

Heartland's extraordinary videographer, Douglas D. Mills (the "D" is for Danger), was harnessed with ropes and hoisted up by the crew to the top of the tree to get a shot of Mama bear and her cubs inside the cavity.

He positioned himself, and when he spotted

[15]

Dr. Mike Pelton assesses how to hoist videographer Doug Mills up a tree.

Doug learns he has to climb ninety-foot tree.

Doug hoisted up the tree.

the bear, he yelled down for the camera. "It's too dark," he hollered back, "send up a light." It had taken an hour with four or five grad students helping to get to this point.

With the heavy camera right in front of the cavity, he leaned over into the dark hole and the lens cap fell off, hitting Mama Bear in the nose! She was two feet from the lens of the camera and Doug. When the cap hit her, she opened one eye and winked at Doug! Yikes.

Doug got the shot, as he always did, but you couldn't tell squat even with a light. A black bear in a dark hole looks like a black coat in a closet. To complete the footage, we had to hire Donelle Dewitt, WBIR's graphic artist, to draw a picture of a bear in a den, ninety feet up a tree. That's rule number one. You can't do a TV show without showing the animal.

Once, Doug left at 3:00 a.m. with some wildlife people to get black bear footage in the Pisgah National Forest. We didn't see him for three

How to Catch a Bear in the Woods

We heard about the effort to start a black bear reintroduction program in the Big South Fork Natural Wild and Scenic River Area on the Cumberland Plateau. At that time, the Big South Fork didn't have its own bear population.

The National Park had plenty of bears, maybe fourteen hundred or so. "Sure, you can have a few of our bears. Then, everybody will have bears!" That's the way wildlife managers think in Washington D.C., where decisions like this one are made.

Research says, Mama bears are more likely to stay in the area where their cubs are born. So the plan this day was to take a pregnant female bear from the Great Smoky Mountains, drug her, and move her to the Big South Fork. Then, when she gave birth to her cubs, she would be more likely to stay in the Big South Fork area. That way, we could develop a successful population of bears in the Big South Fork.

Wild animals, however, are never predictable. That's why they're called wild animals. We had a hunch we were in trouble from the get-go on this story.

Doug Mills and I met Jay Clark, a researcher and bear scholar, for an early interview. We did this at Tremont where it was quieter, because the Park had invited a multitude of photographers, videographers, and TV crews from all over the country. We usually went out with Dr. Pelton's people, or roughed it. We could tell this was going to be different.

We were herded into golf carts, driven miles, and instructed to hike down a trail and cross a stream. "You'll see waders there for you to use,"

Doug uses portable light to highlight a black bear.

days. When we came in, there was a tape on our desk labeled, "Unfound Bear." The tape was full of great scenic vistas, beautiful mountain views, forest shots, and acorns; but no bears. You've got to see the animal. The more footage you have of your subject the better the story. That's just the fact of it.

"The more footage you have of your subject the better the story. That's just the fact of it."

The crew interviews a ranger for trail maintenance episode.

the official said. We thought, "Waders? What's this guy talking about?"

Sure enough, when we arrived at the stream, there was a rope tied across it, and four sets of waders on each side of the stream. We thought, "Wow! This is high living." We arranged our gear, put on the waders, and crossed the stream without getting our footsies wet. We took off the waders and left them for the next soul who happened to wander by.

Hiking on, we saw a large crowd gathered on top of a rise. When we reached the knoll, we found dozens of camera people and official-looking park rangers whom we'd never seen before. Doing as much work over as many years as we did, we'd come to know most of the wildlife specialists and rangers that worked for the National Park.

Suddenly, from a hand-held loud speaker, we hear a shrill sound: "WOULD THE HEARTLAND CREW PLEASE STEP FORWARD." As Doug and I moved forward, the little guy with the speaker pointed it right at us and screamed, "YOU'LL BE THE POOL PHOTOGRAPHERS. PLEASE FOLLOW THE RANGER TOWARD THE BEAR."

So we followed this other guy down the ridge. We saw two more rangers, one standing on a limb twenty feet off the ground. The loud speaker guy hollered again, "THEY ARE THE POOL PHOTOGRAPHERS. THE VIDEO THEY SHOOT WILL BE SHARED BY ALL OF YOU. YOU'LL ALL GET COPIES FOR YOUR STORIES. DON'T WORRY. PLEASE BE PATIENT."

Whoa! This was certainly news to us. We looked at each other, shrugged, and positioned ourselves. We didn't have a clue what was going on.

Doug tried to get his feet positioned where he could get a shot of the twenty-year-old ranger, standing on a limb of a huge oak tree. The ranger had a fold-out pole, like a giant carpenter's ruler, the kind that adjusts out to about three feet. Except this guy's pole when fully extended was about twelve feet long. On the end he'd secured a hypodermic needle loaded with tranquilizers. He jammed the pole down the hollowed-out tree like he was digging a well.

We watched him with the camera rolling. He looked at us and saw we were shooting, and in a loud whisper said, "I'm darting the bear now. I'm drugging the bear." Then, from about a hundred and fifty yards away, we heard over the loud speaker: "HE'S DARTING THE BEAR! NOW WE'RE DARTING AND DRUGGING THE BEAR."

Doug smiled and continued to point the camera at the guy in the tree. Finally, he stopped jamming the pole, looked at us, and whispered, "We've

darted the bear," and from far away we heard: "WE'VE DARTED THE BEAR!"

The ranger said to us, "It'll take about ten minutes before the drug takes effect, so you can take it easy for a few minutes." Doug moved the camera angle down a bit and relaxed. Just as we started to rest, we saw a funny look come over the young ranger's face. His eyes got big as saucers. We heard this screeetch, screeetch, scratching, just like the sound of fingernails on a blackboard. Suddenly, the ranger leapt into the air, like he's flying out of the tree! One moment he's standing there, the next he has this terrified look of panic and he's airborne.

At about that instant, the bear shot out of the tree like an exploding volcano. It happened in one blur of motion. The bear hit the tree on the way down and landed about twenty feet from the tree.

The crew and volunteers prepare to set out on "Stream Restoration" project.

National Park bear is drugged and moved to the Big South Fork. I'm not much help!

Bears don't read the script. They don't care how far you've come to take their picture or how important you are. They're just bears and they act like bears.

As we headed back to the Tremont Environmental Educational Center, it became clear we'd have to go to plan B, or even plan C, if they had one. Plan A was the easy one. That bear was close and it got away. Many of the photographers and photojournalists had planes to catch, deadlines to meet. The Park had lured media from all over the country to help tell this story. It's a pity it didn't work out.

The next day at 8:00 a.m., twenty people met on the southern side of the Park, near Parsons Branch Road. We hiked five miles up Parsons, but this time, Kim Delozier, head of Wildlife Resources for the Park, was with us. He successfully darted a bear. He used a chain saw to cut the top of the tree off, so we could get to the bear. It was difficult to pull that bear up out of the stump, even without the tree above it.

Hiking out with the bear balanced on a two-wheel gurney, or stretcher gizmo, wasn't easy. It's a difficult balancing act with a three-hundred-and-fifty-pound bear, even with a lot of help. The bear was doctored and its health checked before it was taken out of the Park.

We did all of this before darkness fell, including driving the bear one hundred and fifty miles to the Big South Fork, and getting it safely into a secure cave, its new home. Soon, she would have her cubs. Hopefully, she would stay with them and begin a new chapter in the tale of restoring black bears to the Eastern United States. Now, there would be black bears in the Big South Fork, too.

In less than a week, that same bear was found up a tree on the front lawn of Blount Memorial

It rolled two or three times and, faster than the wink of an eye, disappeared over the next ridge and was gone.

The entire scene played out in no more than two seconds. It was like one of those toys where the little man on the trapeze flips over and back as you squeeze the sticks. It was the fastest thing I've ever seen. I turned to Doug and said, half kidding, "Did you get that?" Nobody could "get that." I didn't know what else to say. I was stupefied. Doug was confused. It was like we'd seen an alien or something. It was unnatural. If I hadn't seen it, I wouldn't have believed it.

To our right, the guy with the walkie talkie started screaming, "The bear's in the woods! The bear's loose in the woods! Repeat: She's out of the tree and gone!" Then, we hear, "THE BEAR'S OUT OF THE TREE AND SHE'S IN THE WOODS RUNNING. SHE'S RUNNING AWAY. OH, NO. SHE'S RUNNING AWAY!"

Hospital, in Maryville. She'd traveled all the way back toward her home and almost made it. She was a Smoky Mountain bear, and that's where she wanted to be.

Ever since this experience, I've had new respect for black bears. They're incredibly strong, so strong a baby bear can rip open a metal Coke machine. They're fast, too, like I've tried to describe. And because they're wild animals, they never do exactly what we think they'll do.

Up on Mt. Sterling

Lenny Garver is the mountain mailman up on Mt. Sterling. He was born there, grew up there, and knows everyone who lives there. It's a nice job for him, and he's good at it.

The mail arrives first at the post office in Cocke County, Tennessee. Then, he delivers it to folks who live along the road that leads up the mountain. Most of them are across the state line in North Carolina. So, Lenny collects mail in one state and delivers it in another. It sounds odd, but that's just the way it works best there.

Lenny's a funny elf of a man. He travels the gravel road from the foot of the mountain, where the post office is, all the way to the top of Mt. Sterling. His customers live all along it. Near the top of Mt. Sterling, the National Park begins at about four thousand feet elevation. There are no residents living in the Park. The road, however, continues over the top of Mt. Sterling down into Cataloochie on the other side, and on into Bryson City, North Carolina.

This is one spectacular photographic opportunity. As you drive this road, near the top of Mt. Sterling at six thousand feet elevation, the view is stunning. It's one of the highest peaks on this side of the Great Smoky Mountains National Park. You're in North Carolina the entire time. The last farm, the last piece of private property before you enter the Park, is one of the most beautiful places you've never seen.

It belongs to a man we'll call Mr. Steve Francis. But you've never seen this picture, this farm, this view. That's because Mr. Francis won't let us take a picture of it. It's his farm. We didn't understand it. In all our years *Heartlanding*, we've rarely been told not to take a picture. Usually, it's the other way. Folks want you to take a picture of their land. They're proud of it.

This particular farmstead is spectacularly gorgeous. The barns, and there are several, all have old stone foundations that stretch upwards of ten feet. Some are two and three story barns nestled snugly into the steep mountain terrain. It's a sloped mountainside. The stone keeps the outbuildings from rotting when the deep snows come and stay for most of the winter. It looks like Austria or the Alps.

Even though Lenny asked Mr. Francis for us on two different occasions, we still struck out. This old mountain man didn't want to talk to us and he didn't want us to take any pictures "a-tall." We thought we could change his mind if we came with Lenny and asked in person. This was our third trip. Maybe it would be the charm, as they say. We lucked out and caught sight of him for the first time. He was lean and small and had a full beard to his belt. It would be so cool if we could talk to him!

Mr. Francis met Lenny at his mailbox. It was as good a place as any to approach him. So, very tentatively, we edged a bit closer. Now, he'd already told us twice, via Lenny, not to take any pictures of his farm. But there he was, in his overalls and long grey beard. We had to try one more time. If

Videographer, Doug Mills, during one of his Fu Manchu periods.

Left: **Hal Watson on Texas.**
Right: **Horse riders in the Park.**

we were very, very nice to him, maybe we could get him to talk to us on camera, too.

"Boy, it sure is beautiful up here," I said. Man, did that sound lame or what! "Mr. Francis?" I said. He looked up from the mail he was thumbing through. He hadn't said a word. He hadn't even acknowledged our presence, even with Doug standing there with camera resting on his shoulder and careful not to point it at anything.

"Can I ask you, Mr. Francis, please? How come you won't let us photograph this beautiful place, this spectacular farm you've got up here so high? Why won't you talk to us?"

Lenny looked at us. Then, he looked at Mr. Francis, who even with the long beard, didn't appear to be over fifty years old. He was wiry and, maybe, weighed a hundred and fifty pounds. But to work this place, it had to be a hundred and fifty pounds of pure mountain gristle.

He looked up, started towards me, and got right up in my face. He looked me straight in the eye and said: "If'n I let you take your pictures up here of all this—he motioned to the view over the mountain across his farm—you'll put it on the TV, right?" His pronunciation of "TV" was more like Teee Veee! He carried the "E" sounds way long and sarcastic, obviously showing disdain for the whole idea of that vulgar box called television.

"Yes, sir," I said.

He continued his point, "And then all them people from Canadeeee that took off and come down to Florideee, then they'll all see it, right? How beautiful it is here. Huh? Won't they?"

"Yes, sir," I said again. "Some of them will."

"Then, all them people from Canadeeee and Florideeee'll see it, how beautiful it is here. And then they'll aaall, all them people from Canadeeee and Florideeee will come up here and then, they'll jest light!"

His arms were both extended as he finished. As he said the word "light," he crossed his arms very fast and then let them down. It was like mimicking a duck settling on a pond or an umpire judging the runner safe at the plate.

We never did get any pictures of Mr. Francis or his farm. We thought and talked about it all the way back to the station. He was right, too.

Lenny Garver's Tale of How to Catch a Bear

Lenny Garver had a bear tale to tell. He told this one for the truth. Interestingly, a month ago, traveling with Kim Delozier, we met an old retired ranger who happened to have worked the Mt. Sterling area. He knew Lenny and knows for a fact this story is true.

"It happened," Lenny said, "along that little old road that runs over the mountain into Cataloochie and on into Bryson City."

If you've ever driven it, you know it's a doozey. You really need a four-wheel drive vehicle, maybe a tough high-axel van. The *Heartland* truck made it, but it's a tough Ford 150, although without four-wheel drive. I wouldn't try it in a van.

I wouldn't try it in a car either. It is one lane most of the way. It's overgrown, wild country, too. Hemlocks, big oaks, dark forests, wild mountains, it's thick in there. There's a hundred years of rhododendron and laurel growing on either side of the old gravel and dirt road. In some parts, there are tight curves and drop-offs. The road is all rutted up. You bounce up and down as it goes around and through the shallow creeks you have to cross. There's no other way.

I tried to go into Cataloochie once this way on a Sunday drive with the family. It took an hour and a half to travel about twelve miles. Then, it took another hour and a half to drive back. The family wasn't very happy about it a–tall.

Lenny giggled as he told us his story. He said, "One time, as a teenage boy, I and three of my buddies from in and around here were heading to a big shindig, a dance in Bryson City and boy, were we excited!"

Black bear walking away.

Jeep damaged by black bear.

He talked his dad into letting him drive their new car. "It was pretty new," he said. "It was a 1948 Ford, but it had four doors. We called it, 'the black beauty.' We were proud of that car, too, especially Daddy.

"Anyway, we were coming over the mountain that night. My three friends and I were feeling awful good about everything. Coming through that thick laurel, we saw two big bears in there. They were close to the road, too. After the dance, on the way back home, we said, 'Hey, let's catch them big bears! Daddy will be so proud of us.'

"So, on the way out of Bryson City, we stopped and pooled what money we had left and got a steak. We thought we'd catch those bears with that steak! Right where we saw those bears coming over through there, we pulled the car to a stop and opened the trunk and tied a little string to the steak. We hung that steak there dangling for them bears.

"We'd set a trap in Daddy's car for the bear! Then, we waited," he said. "We laid there for about forty minutes or so, 'bout half asleep, when sure enough here come that bear. And he got to sniffing around the trunk of Daddy's car. And just like we planned, we jumped out of the thicket, pushed that bear into the trunk of Daddy's car, and slammed the trunk shut. 'We got him!' we hollered. Ha. We caught that bear, just like we said we would.

"Well, sir, we thought how proud Daddy was gonna be that we brung home a big bear. I was thinking just such a thing when we heard this roaring and a-snortin'! And up through the trunk of Daddy's car, here come that ole bear. He comes right up through the back seat, I'm telling you! And he was a-rippin' and a-roarin.'

"You never saw four doors a-flyin' open any faster in your life! We four fellers jumped out of that car and just left them doors a-swingin' there. We left the car a-runnin', too! Had to! The bear, he tore that car all up. He come right up through the trunk and tore the whole back seat out."

Lenny just shook his head, remembering. "Tore the whole front seat up, too. Tore it all to pieces. It was the worst whippin' I ever got. Daddy was so mad at me for lettin' that bear tear up his new car. Ha!"

He looked up. "We sure didn't eat that bear. He got away! We didn't eat that steak either."

CHAPTER 4

Adventures on LeConte

Uncharted Territory

There are many good reasons why something like *The Heartland Series* had never been attempted before in our market. Actually, there were programs similar to ours, just not as big. We had an entire team committed to it.

Usually, local TV stations can't afford to send three people out to do one story. To feature the natural beauty of an area and its people is a luxury. To do it takes three people: a cameraman, a sound person, and a field producer. You also need someone to edit the stories.

When we started, we used three-quarter-inch tape. The sound recorder and the camera were separate pieces of equipment, connected by a cable. The recorder was a metal box, one-by-two feet square, and it was carried over your shoulder by a strap. This box recorded both video and sound. If we were using more than two channels because a lot of people were talking, we often carried a mixer to blend the audio. The sound person had to carry both recorder and mixer.

It didn't take us long to learn that one of our biggest strengths was our use of the natural sounds of nature; "nat sounds" we called them. Nature sounds are richly appealing. Capturing the sounds of the wind in the mountains, a screeching peregrine falcon in flight, a gurgling, pristine, bubbling brook, or a running stream put the audience in the wilds with us.

That recorder weighed about twelve to fifteen pounds. It seemed even heavier when you lugged it around, unless you were on a horse, or in a rubber raft, wagon, or canoe. Carrying that damn recorder cut into your shoulder after a mile or two. You couldn't carry it in a pack. It wouldn't fit.

If you were on a horse, we thought, you could rest it on the saddle horn, balance it there. But we found out the hard way that didn't always work. Once, I was balancing the recorder on my saddle horn when my horse took off and flipped me. But I managed to save the recorder. It was cushioned by my stomach. It nearly knocked me out, but we managed to finish the shoot.

Doug always carried the camera, always. It weighed about fifteen pounds, maybe more—I don't want to think about how much it weighed. A lot, that's how much.

Mt. LeConte on Horseback

It was our very first trip to LeConte in 1984. We thought it would be a good idea to take horses and

Loading up for winter on LeConte.

to let the horses carry the gear while we rode the horses. Boy, we thought that was a good idea. We were awful proud of ourselves for thinking of that! The trouble was the Park no longer allowed horses on many of the LeConte trails, and none of the horse operations would rent us horses.

The lodge was using llamas to carry supplies up and garbage down. What were we going to do? We wanted no part of a seven mile hike up Mt. LeConte, carrying all our gear.

So we turned to Hal Watson for help. Hal just happens to be about the best actor I ever met, even though he had absolutely no training. He'd already worked at the station twenty years or more and had tons of experience in master control and as a director. He also moonlighted as an Assistant Deputy Sheriff of Sevier County.

Five-mile horseback ride to Walnut Bottoms.

Lucky for us, he raised and trained horses. "Sure, boys," he said, "I'll get you some horses." He did, too, but most of them had never been on a mountain trail before.

We met at around 7:30 a.m. at the Cherokee Orchard Trail. We planned to go up Cherokee Orchard and the next day return on the Trillium Gap Trail. It was 9:00 a.m. before all of the equipment needed for a two-day shoot was tied securely to the horses.

We were just about to mount up and yell, "Head 'em up and move 'em out," when we heard a huge commotion. It was Hal wrestling and cussing with his mare. As soon as she took her first step, all hell broke loose!

The tripod swayed back and hit the rump of Hell's Bitch, Widow Maker, Demon, or whatever she was called. When the tripod kicked her butt, she started bucking and jumping up and down like at a rodeo. She was fully packed, too. Every time the horse hit the ground another piece of equipment went flying off into the woods.

The horse kept bucking higher and higher until she went right up to the top of a sapling and straddled it. The tree bent over double, and that horse looked like one of those singing crows in the Walt Disney movie, *Dumbo, the Flying Elephant*.

We couldn't believe it. I remember thinking, "Maybe I should clap." It was that good a show. We didn't know it then, but we were just getting started. It was awful going up the mountain on those horses. We found out they hated each other.

For some reason, if they moved closer than about fifteen feet, the horses would start kicking and biting one another—snorting, stomping, and jumping around. It got to be downright dangerous. On the way up, we tried to grab a few shots of the horses traveling. You know, going by the camera with the mountains off in the distant background. Nothing difficult, we thought.

Doug set up the camera thirty yards ahead of us, but those horses started bucking and kicking when we started moving, and the poor terrified riders held on for dear life. When we finally made it by the camera, we stopped and looked around at Doug. He just looked up, smiled, and said, "Okay, let's do it again!"

We looked at one another and yelled back, "We can't do it again. We couldn't do it the first time!" Imagine trying to turn around eight horses, loaded with gear and inexperienced riders, on a mountain trail, three feet wide with a four-thousand-feet drop-off on one side. We did it once, though, for Dougie.

My horse actually backed off the trail. Like a dog-paddling horse, and with dirt flying everywhere, it nearly fell one thousand feet, with me

The indomitable Hal Watson and friend.

Adventures on LeConte [27]

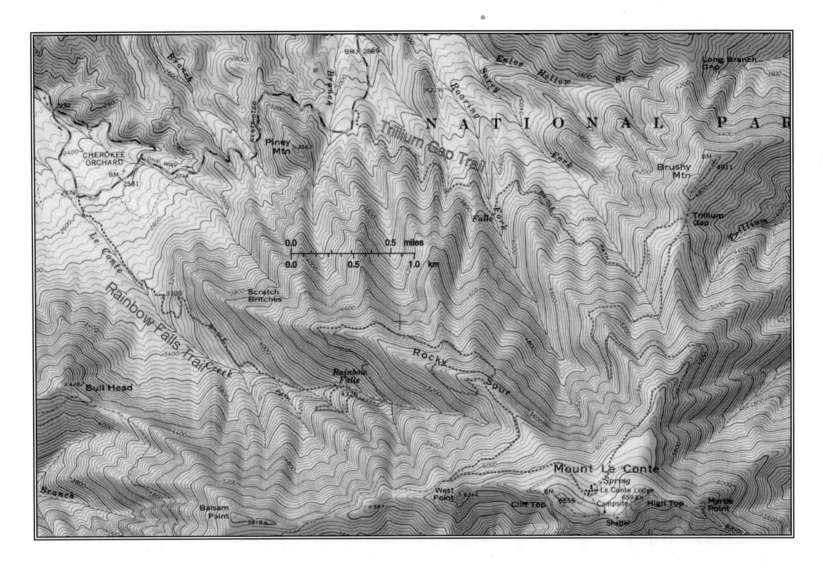

LeConte horseback route—Rainbow Falls up, Trillium Gap down.

holding on to its neck. This happened at least once to almost all of us on that trail—those non-trail horses stepping into the abyss.

Eight long, exhausting, terrifying hours later, we arrived at LeConte Lodge atop Mt. LeConte. Doug rode ahead to set up the camera by the horse railings where you could still tie up your horse. He wanted to get a shot of us riding up, dismounting, and tying off.

Doug hollers, "Ready," and we started forward towards him. At the precise moment when all our horses were all lined up, framed for the shot, my horse, Knucklehead, slammed me into a big fir tree, pinning my leg against it. Then, he started twisting around while my foot was caught in the stirrup, bent double. "AAAAHHHIIII!" I screamed in pain. Doug just cut off the audio. He couldn't stand it. We stumbled through the rest of the shot, tears running down my face. The show must go on no matter what, somebody once said. I thought I'd broken my leg.

We arrived hungry, tired, bedraggled, and sore, still shaking from so many near misses on the way up. Apart from mice running all over the equipment, getting into our shoes, beds, and in our ears, it was a wonderful trip.

Our hosts at the lodge, Tim Line and his wife, Lisa, and their crew, were very kind to us and hospitable. We even met and interviewed Herrick Brown, who managed the lodge after Paul Adams first cobbled it together.

On the way back down the mountain we took the Trillium Gap Trail. We rode the horses very slowly and carefully along a wide trail covered with leaves, trying to keep plenty of room between them. It was October, clear and crisp with a beautiful, bright-blue sky above us.

Suddenly, the trail opened up, wide enough for a wagon, and all the horses took off in a dead run. With no warning, we were flying down that mountain. I don't know why. I guess they knew they were heading back to the barn. They careened one way, then another, back and forth, as they ran down the mountain.

I could see Doug up ahead on the horse in front of me. He had the camera, cradling it in his lap, trying to keep it secured against the saddle horn. His butt was bouncing up and down. I was sure he was going to fly off, but he never did. None of us did. We just flew down the mountain.

We were still in shock when we staggered into the station the next day. When Steve saw us, the first thing he asked was, "Did you get a wide shot of the mountain?" Huh? We looked at each other. Oh, no! We'd forgotten to get a wide shot of the mountain we'd just spent two days climbing.

Roscoe Stinnett, Doug, and a young me assemble tripod, camera, and recorder. Note cable used to connect recorder and camera.

A few weeks later, we ran the first of those stories, "Climbing LeConte." The next week, we ran the other, "LeConte Lodge." Another lesson learned. No matter where you are or what you're doing, always get a wide shot of it. "How can you do two shows on Mt. LeConte and not shoot Mt. LeConte?" Steve asked us. I don't know, but that's what we did.

Equipment Overload

In addition to the camera and the recorder, the tripod was another heavy piece of equipment that went on every shoot. It was absolutely necessary. Doug puts the camera on it. It steadies the shots for a pan or a zoom, whatever.

Our tripod was a good metal one. It weighed ten pounds and on any hike would easily cut into your shoulder. If we were on horseback, we

In winter especially, we also had to carry gloves, scarves, hats, rain gear, and flashlights! Hey, it's good to have a flashlight, too.

Margaret's Long Dark Walk

Margaret Stevenson was an amazing lady. She liked to hike up Mt. LeConte. In fact, at eighty-two, she had probably hiked up that mountain more than any other living human being. When we were lucky enough to go with her on the Alum Cave Trail, she'd already hiked it five hundred and ninety-eight times! She hiked it seven hundred and nineteen times before she wasn't able to go any more. She was in tremendous physical shape and usually hiked Mt. LeConte every week.

We wanted to do a show with Margaret. We talked to her beforehand, trying to prepare her. For the show we just wanted to talk about hiking to the top of Mt. LeConte. We didn't really need to go all the way up there, or want to, either.

Andy Ramsey was gripping for us then. He was the smallest man ever to do that job, but he was tough and strong. He was maybe twenty-one years old and weighed about a hundred and forty pounds. He never complained that the job was too hard or that he was tired. Andy was inventive and fun to have with us.

On all the *Heartland* shoots, the grip had the hardest physical job. Each time we stopped for a break, we'd ask Andy how he felt. Margaret was fine. She kept going and going and going, like the Energizer Bunny! We were struggling, but we finished what we needed to shoot, and it was still early, maybe 3:00 p.m.

We had our shots of Margaret alone, of her hiking, coming around a mountain with seven rows of mountains behind her. They were great

At top: The Heartland crew taking in the view while climbing LeConte in the snow. *Below:* Jack Huff, the developer of LeConte Lodge

would tie it behind the saddle like a blanket or a bedroll.

It wouldn't break down any shorter than thirty-six inches or so. It was bulky and awkward but you didn't want to keep unpacking it, so it had to be carried by hand. On a five mile hike, it was a nasty piece of equipment to lug around. I know. For twenty-five years, it was usually my job to carry it.

Big square heavy metal batteries fit on the back of the camera to power it. Each battery weighed about five pounds. Often we needed four or five on a shoot. We spread those around. It was like carrying a six-pack of metal shot puts.

The combined weight of this equipment was considerable. You can understand why it took three or four people. The camera weighed twenty pounds, the recorder about eighteen pounds, and the tripod ten pounds. Add to this, five batteries, three or four tapes, water, and lunch. You've got a load, thirty to forty pounds of gear per person.

shots, beautiful shots. We lucked out and got shots of her meeting hiking friends on the trail. "It's a wrap!" We didn't need to go all the way up and there wasn't enough time. But Margaret wanted to go all the way up. I guess I can't blame her, so we just kept going.

At Alum Cave Bluffs we asked Andy if he could go a little farther. It was about 4:00 p.m. "It's only a little farther," Margaret kept saying. So, we went on, all the way to the top. Exhausted, at the lodge we sat down and had a cup of that wonderful hot chocolate they have up there. We rested for ten minutes and spoke with Tim Line and his wife. We tried to get our minds right for the six-mile trek back down.

Sitting there at 5:00 p.m., or maybe 5:30, we knew the sun was about to set. Uh, oh! It would be pitch dark before we could make it halfway down. We shouldn't have been in this predicament. We'd tried to avoid it. We didn't even have a flashlight, but there wasn't anything else we could do. So we hitched up our britches, turned around, and started back down the mountain, fast. It was like trying to get inside the castle with Dracula hot on your trail, before the sun goes down!

Doug walked on one side of Margaret toward the mountain, and I walked on the other side of her to keep her from falling into the stream below. It was dark as death. We couldn't see anything. That's the way we traveled, all the way down the mountain, arm and arm, together, the three of us. Andy Ramsey was behind us, I guess. I was too tired to care.

It was extremely dangerous going through that Arch Rock section below Alum Cave without any light. Pitch black, blind dark. For a while, every hundred meters we'd flick a Bic lighter for a few seconds to get our bearings. But we found it actually hurt rather than helped our ability to see in the dark.

So we just walked blindly, taking tiny little steps. Like Dorothy, the Tin Man, and the Scarecrow on the yellow brick road, we walked all the way down from Mt. LeConte with Andy following behind. It was 11:00 p.m. and cold when we finally made it to the truck.

We carried flashlights with us after that. Andy made it all right, too. He went on to a successful career as a hard-working music composer, even winning a Grammy. He now has a family and teaches at Belmont College in Nashville.

"It's only a little farther."
—**Margaret Stevenson on one of her seven hundred and nineteen LeConte hikes.**

Adventures on LeConte

The Happy Hiker outdoor guide service and the crew before the hike.

Winter on Mt. LeConte

The Heartland Series was always an outdoor, on-location, natural world show, particularly in the beginning. We went places and took the camera on-location with us, documenting things never before seen by people in our region. As an example, prior to the *Series,* no one had gone to the top of Mt. LeConte to make a video in winter.

We'd climbed LeConte, shooting episodes up there five times, but on this particular trip, the idea was to shoot winter on Mt. LeConte. It was a bad idea, I can tell you; whoever suggested it didn't have to go up there with us! At least we had the foresight to go by The Happy Hiker outdoor guide service in Gatlinburg, and invited those pros to go with us to help keep us alive. Tom Bosch, Lee Lewis, Mike Povia, and Harold Welsh went with us and looked after us.

We met early at their store about 8:00 a.m. and immediately they insisted I couldn't go! "What do you mean, I can't go," was my reply.

"Not with those boots you're wearing, you can't."

"So, the sole of my boot flaps a little when I walk. What's that gonna hurt?"

Right away, they put me in a pair of brand new $145-boots that the station had to pay for. And, I might add, they were not happy about that. My feet hurt the entire trip. I developed blisters on my

Being fitted for new boots at The Happy Hiker.

blisters wearing those new boots, but that was the least of our problems.

The Happy Hikers also gave each of us a pair of "cramp-ons" for our boots. I'd never seen crampons before. They're like ice cleats. They strap to your boots like old-time roller skates—the kind you needed a key to tighten. We thought they were for mountain climbing, like the Himalayas or climbing the Matterhorn. They're actually for walking on ice. "Hey! What the hell do we need these for?" was our reaction.

We absolutely had no idea what we were in for. It's a good thing, too. If we'd known, we would have turned around right then and headed for the house. It was 1992 when we went on this hairbrained shoot. When we left Knoxville, it was thirty-two degrees with two inches of dusty snow on the ground. When we finally neared the top of the mountain, it was twelve degrees and there was nine inches of snow.

On the way up, everything was already frozen. The cable that keeps you from falling off the mountain around Alum Cave Bluffs was covered with two or three inches of ice. You couldn't hold it. We needed those cramp-ons, all right!

It was freezing. I've never been so cold. Doug Mills wore his standard winter gear: blue jeans with long-johns underneath. Because of the snow, he wore a rubber rain suit over his blue jeans to keep the moisture out. The problem was the plastic

Adventures on LeConte

Standard *Heartland* gear: tripod, camera, recorder, batteries, mics, etc., plus lunch!

rain suit kept the perspiration in. We were all carrying forty-pound packs or more and, in spite of the cold, sweated profusely on the way up. It was another hard, physical climb.

What happened to Doug was that all his perspiration got trapped inside. It completely covered him between his blue jeans and shirts, and his outer suit. Nobody knew it, not even Doug, until after the eight hour climb. By the time we finally reached the top, Doug wasn't looking too good. I'd never seen him look worse.

The moisture couldn't escape, so it froze inside his plastic rain suit. By the time we made it to the top, Doug was turning white! We'd noticed it earlier, but thought he was just tired. When we took off his rain suit inside the lodge, Doug was covered in ice. He looked like an abominable snowman. A thick inch of ice had accumulated around him, coating his whole body. He couldn't move. Past being white, he was now turning blue. We immediately put him to bed in the Lodge's big sleeping room. We put six big wool blankets on him, and let all the mice run over and around him while he slept. He couldn't feel them!

The lodge had no heat because it was shut down for the winter. It was about 10:00 that night before we got the stove working in the kitchen, and could feel some heat. Combined with the warmth provided by the propane heater, we managed to raise the temperature to a scorching thirty-five degrees. We finally ate something.

That night the wind blew and it snowed. The wind chill plummeted to fifty-six below. The next day, with Doug up and, surprisingly, feeling better, we went out in twenty-four degrees below zero weather and shot two shows. It was so cold we couldn't stay outside more than five or six minutes without the camera freezing up. Each time we went outside, the camera fogged up, both inside and out.

I had to do a wrap or two out there in that cold. Linda wrote it, and I tried to memorize the lines. Doug, of course, was shooting the video. Whew! It was cold. I was stuttering badly and my teeth were rattling. Doug had me standing in a two-foot snow drift, trying to talk: "I'm B, B, Ba, Ba, Bill La, La, La, Landry and it's c, ca, ca, cold up here!" It was so cold up there that day that when I finally got my words out, they just froze solid in the air! Then, plop! They just fell down into the snow bank and disappeared.

Tim Line's people say, later that spring, when my words thawed out, the employees of the lodge could hear me hollerin' all over the mountain. Most of the above story is true. Anyway, I'm telling it for the truth.

Cold, tired, and hungry.

Eating at LeConte Lodge.

LeConte cabins in the snow.

A cold crew, good and ready to leave LeConte.

CHAPTER 5

Nature's Guides and Unlikely Explorers

Maynard Ledbetter and the Bees

On a beautiful spring day, we returned to Cades Cove to visit our old friend, seventy-nine-year-old Maynard Ledbetter. Maynard grew up in Cades Cove and was featured in our very first year of the *Series*. We were looking for the location where Maynard's house stood.

Retracing his boyhood trails, he found the exact spot where he grew up. Then, he looked around and found his mother's rose bushes. I'll never forget what Maynard said that day. "These are mother's old rose bushes. That's all that's left of where we grew up. Mother's old rose bushes. That's all that's left."

Maynard always repeated everything he said at least twice. Once, he was telling me how to wash a quilt. "They used to wash their quilts in the creek," he said. "That's a good place to ranse quilts, in the creek. Just wade out there in the creek. And ranse 'em in the creek. That's a good place to ranse quilts in the creek. Just wade out there and ranse 'em in the creek."

That first episode with Maynard was called "The Homecoming." And he became a very good and unique friend from then on. Maybe five years later, we needed to talk to Maynard about the Cove. We were working on the thirty minute feature "Cades Cove—The Homeplace." Maynard was a big part of it. So we took him into Cades Cove from his home in Townsend.

We had to drive him because they took his license away. Riding with Maynard was an adventure, particularly driving that narrow road into the Cove. He had this habit of driving on the left hand side of the road. It made him mad as a hornet when the rangers stopped him.

Near the end of his driving days, this happened often. I was riding with him once when a young ranger pulled him over and made him get out of the car. He knew Maynard—everybody did. He was respectful and simply reminded Maynard, "Stay over on your side of the road, Mr. Ledbetter." Maynard mumbled something under his breath that none of us could hear.

This day we were in Cades Cove looking for a place to do the interview with Maynard. Hey, we thought, this looks like a good open spot. So, we

[37]

Mann Ledbetter, Maynard's father, (*second from right*) at hunting cabin.

set him down on a great big stump, right in the middle of an open field. It was perfect, right on his daddy's land, Mann Ledbetter's old land in the upper end of the Cove.

It wasn't long before we noticed yellow jackets flying around him. Maynard saw them, too, and started grabbing at them. He snatched them with his hands, pinched them, and killed them. It was like swatting a fly to him. Doug had the camera rolling.

He kept pinching at them and squeezing them if he caught them, and he caught a lot of them. But, he didn't get stung or seem to mind much at all. Finally, it dawned on us, Doug, Linda, and me. We had sat Maynard down on the middle of a yellow jacket's nest to do an interview!

Maynard Ledbetter and my son Jack in Cades Cove.

Dr. Aaron "Jack" Sharp

Throughout his career, Professor Emeritus of Botany at the University of Tennessee, Dr. Aaron Sharp introduced me and thousands of other students, hikers, and outdoor enthusiasts to the Great Smoky Mountains National Park.

He began work at the university in the early 1930s and never left, although he had many offers and opportunities. "Why should I?" he often said, "I've the greatest botanical experimental station in the world right here within an hour's drive of my office—the Great Smoky Mountains National Park."

When Dr. Sharp started looking for a career, he considered going into the seminary. This is a fairly common thing among botanists. There's a close correlation between faith or spirituality and the study of nature and plants.

When I began working at Channel 10 in 1984, Selma Myers, an avid hiker and wildflower enthusiast, told me to call up Jack Sharp on the phone. "He'll teach you about the Smokies," she said. "Sure, he'd love to introduce you to the wonders and joys of the Great Smoky Mountains."

"I can't call Dr. Jack Sharp," I thought to myself. "He's a highly respected professor emeritus of botany. I'm just a TV guy trying to learn something about the plants and animals of the Park." But Aunt Selma made me call him.

"Could you show me something of the plant life of the Smoky Mountains?" I said, timidly. I must have sounded like a kid asking for his first date.

Dr. Sharp said, "When do you want to go?" We went that same day, even though it was raining. I picked him up at his University of Tennessee office on the hill. He sounded like a kid in a candy store.

Dr. Aaron Sharp teaching at the Wildflower Pilgrimage.

We felt awful. We tried to apologize for putting him in such a predicament. But Maynard just kept pinching the heads off the yellow jackets and said, "I don't know what it is, but I'll soon have 'em all kilt out."

Later, when I related this story to his granddaughter, she reminded me that he raised bees all the time. "So that's it!" I thought to myself. He raised bees and didn't think a thing about getting stung. He was probably used to it. She said he was. But we tried not to interview anyone in a yellow jacket's nest again.

Nature's Guides and Unlikely Explorers

Dr. Sharp and me around 1987.

He was about eighty-two then, but acted like he was fifty-five. We drove out of town through Sevierville, then Gatlinburg, and up into the park. It was my first of a thousand journeys to Clingmans Dome, the highest point in the Smoky Mountains.

As we neared the top, we entered the spruce/fir forest, where balsam firs and red spruce trees are the dominant species. They grow only at a relatively high elevation, maybe three thousand feet above sea level. Gatlinburg is about eighteen hundred feet.

Dr. Sharp was telling me stories when he abruptly exclaimed, "Stop the car!" I'd been asking how to tell the difference between a spruce tree and a balsam fir. We were near the top of the mountain at about six thousand feet. Dr. Sharp wore that same old grey raincoat he always wore. He jumped out of the car above Morton's Overlook, near Newfound Gap, and disappeared down into the forest. He was gone!

I sat there dumbfounded as the windshield wipers slapped back and forth. I thought, "Damn, I might've killed Dr. Sharp. Boy, there'll be hell to pay. The headlines will read: 'Professor emeritus disappears over edge of mountain!' 'He just jumped over the edge. I couldn't stop him,' a saddened Bill Landry is quoted as saying."

But just as fast as he left, he came back. He jumped into the car, water dripping from his coat and hat. He held up these two bristly pine twigs. One was from a spruce and the other from a fir.

"See!" he said, beaming. "The needles of the balsam fir tree grow out and up, like a fir. They're softer and more substantive. The red spruce needles are flatter, more on a single plane, like a hemlock." I've never forgotten the difference.

Dr. Sharp never minded telling me the name of the flowers over and over. Once, he spent the entire afternoon showing me the vicious briars and spikes on a plant called the Hercules Club. That's what he called it. It's a plant that's also known as the Devil's Walking Stick, because it's covered with thorns.

Nearly twenty-five years later, my wife and I were driving near Look Rock on the parkway between Townsend and Chilhowee. She was fascinated by this flowering shrub with its profusion of blooms rising high above the plants surrounding it. We stopped, and I got out of the car for a closer look. I was surprised, smiled, and said with confidence, "Hey, that's called a Hercules Club. I recognized the briars and vicious thorns on the stalk."

"How do you know what it's called?" she said.

"Dr. Sharp showed it to me, at least twenty-five years ago, maybe more. I've never seen it in bloom before." I replied.

Jack Sharp has been gone for nearly a decade now and he's still teaching me, as well as probably thousands of his students, too. Isn't that amazing?

Once, he gave me a book called *The Plant Hunters,* describing incredible journeys of John Bartram, William Bartram's father, and others. Dr. Sharp was one of the world's foremost authorities on mosses and lichens. Like Bartram and other plant collectors, he ventured deep into the jungles of Guatemala and Mexico, anywhere in the world where there was a chance to find a new species or identify and collect a rare or unusual one.

A story that Dr. Sharp loved to tell was from one of these journeys. On this particular trip, he was deep in the jungles of Mexico and had been there for more than a week. Half lost, he wandered into a village where everyone thought he was a priest!

He couldn't understand the dialect of these remote people and kept insisting he was a botanist, not a priest. "I'm just collecting plants," he said. "Not trying to save souls!" Nevertheless, the people of the village kept insisting that he give them his blessing.

Jack said the only way he could get away from there was to bless the adults and baptize the children by making the sign of the cross and pouring water across their brows. But he had to say something.

Since he didn't know what a priest said, he recited the Latin names of plants while baptizing the villagers' children. He said, "Abra cadabra, I baptize thee 'terra vibernum,' or 'ilex teleflora,' or 'ilex blanco'."

William Bartram by Charles Willson Peale.

William Bartram

A botanist is an excellent guide to introduce people to a new world. It's for this very reason we chose eighteenth-century explorer, artist, and naturalist William Bartram as the subject for the first *Heartland* episode—the pilot program for the *Series*.

The very first words of the episode are "He was an unlikely explorer," All of us are—you, me, Doug, Sean, Linda, Laura, Steve, our viewers.

Bartram's journey was a fantastic exploration into a new world. From 1772 to 1775, he explored the southern part of what became America, by boat, horse, canoe, and on foot. When he finally arrived back home in Philadelphia, he returned to a brave new world.

It was called the United States of America. When he left Philadelphia, he was a British citizen.

Nature's Guides and Unlikely Explorers [41]

Map depicting Bartram's travels.

But the Revolution was occurring and upon his return he was an American. I often wonder what that must have been like.

Bartram's story is one of real adventure into early America. A friend of Benjamin Franklin's, he was a failure until he did what he always wanted to do—travel into unexplored regions of the southern part of America, collecting and drawing new plants he found growing there.

With the help of his father and a friend, Dr. Fothergill, he sent these back to Europe and sold the seeds and plants through intermediaries to wealthy gardeners in England and Europe.

Much of what is known about wild America in the eighteenth century came from Bartram's great book, *The Travels of William Bartram,* published around 1792. In it, Bartram documented one hundred and forty-four different Native American villages, while crisscrossing what became the South.

In 1984, Jack Sharp gave me a paperback copy of *Bartram's Travels*—it was thrilling and certainly eye opening. Until then, I thought botanists were quiet little scientists that looked through lenses at tiny plants.

But this guy, Bartram, was an amazing character, a heroic character, a cross between Jack Hawkins in *Treasure Island* and a swashbuckling Errol Flynn. He could be played in a film by the likes of John Barrymore, Paul Muni, or Tom Cruise. He was that cool!

You can bet the first section I read of *Bartram's Travels* was where Bartram and a companion came upon the Cherokee maidens picking strawberries in western North Carolina. His "Elysian Fields," he called them. It's pretty racy stuff. Twenty-five years later, we finally made it to the spot where this actually happened and recorded it on camera for a story called "Bartram's Trail." It was as close as Bartram came to our Smoky Mountains.

A Seminole chief gave him his Indian name, "Puc Puggy," because the chief was amused at his penchant for collecting plants. Puc Puggy means "the flower hunter."

It's hard to believe this little known flower hunter's explorations could rival those of such well known historic, dramatic personae as Sir Walter Raleigh, Christopher Columbus, Desoto, Daniel Boone, or Magellan. They do, but few have ever heard of him. At least, he was new to us in 1984. He appeared terribly curious, big-hearted, and relatively fearless. We first read about him in Michael Frome's book, *Strangers in High Places,* a wonderful lyrical introduction to the Great Smoky Mountains.

Bartram was very spiritual. Goodness and tolerance radiates from his writings, his views, and interactions with his fellows. He had a passionate childlike wonder of the natural world. He was an adventurer with deep faith. He loved traveling to new places, meeting new people. He loved people and recognized the good in them.

Coincidentally, that description became the prerequisite job description for working on *The Heartland Series*. First, and most importantly, we had to have a childlike wonder. Focus only on the good. Finally, of course, work like hell!

Dr. Stuart Maher—
Sermons in Stone

Stuart Maher was special—like so many of our subjects; scholars, scientists, historians, or just plain people. He was a senior geologist at Kenwell, Inc. in Maryville, Tennessee. When we first met him, he was in his seventies. It was our first year. We were pretty green, just learning how to do whatever it was we were doing.

Stuart was an expert in the broad field of geology. He always smoked a pipe. No matter what we were talking about or where we were, when it was time to shoot, he'd just put that pipe in his pocket. Oftentimes, we'd smell smoke and cloth burning, and we'd see where his pipe had burned a hole in his pants or singed his shirt below his belt or worse. He didn't care. What a cool dude Stuart Maher was. We loved him.

Whatever he said, you could take to the bank. I never remember him doing a second take unless, of course, I screwed up. He was great on camera. Not just good, I mean great—Richard Attenborough great!

He was gruff, no nonsense, and old-school. He told us about the continents colliding, how sink holes were formed, and how Cades and Tuckaleechee Coves came to be. He explained clearly and succinctly how sandstone from the bottom of an ancient ocean ended up on top of Mt. LeConte, six thousand feet in the air! He was dramatic, powerful, and fun.

Stuart Maher was a great teacher and told great stories. During World War II, he walked through every stream, creek, and small river, from Chattanooga to Kentucky, looking for uranium and other minerals for the U.S. Government. That's where he learned the value of talking to local people about their land, and he taught us the value of doing that.

He would quote the local folklore of a place as easily as he did scientific journal writings. He not only knew the lay of the geologic landscape better than anyone alive, but it was the local history

The incomparable Stuart Maher.

"The land has many secrets. If you listen to it you can learn them, too."
—Sermons in Stone

of a place from the local people's perspective that interested him and endeared him to them.

He once took us to where a meteor landed on a place called Flynn's Lick. We explored with him the formation of the ancient ancestral mountains—that came three hundred and fifty million years BEFORE the Great Smokies were formed. He was just amazing.

When we aired the first two shows with Stuart Maher about the formation of the ancient mountains, including plate tectonics and the continents of North America colliding with Africa, we received a nasty letter at the station which caused a slight stir. Someone wanted to know which one of our employees was around three hundred and fifty million years ago!

The land has many secrets. If you listen to it you can learn them, too. Stuart knew more than his share of them. He called them "Sermons in Stone." The land will tell its story, if you will just listen to it.

Joe Diehl

Joe Diehl was another gifted man who could do anything. He was a prospector, an inventor, coal miner, gold miner, and carpenter. You name it and Joe could do it. His first salaried job, he said, was working for Knoxville Utilities Board during the Depression. He took the job because it was the only opening they had.

It was as a plumber. He worked for a year, was given a raise, and the award for being the best plumber of the year. They asked him at the awards ceremony where he'd learned the trade. Joe said he hadn't done any plumbing until they hired him. That was Joe.

He only weighed a hundred and thirty pounds or so. He taught us how to make fire by friction, twisting a stick in a hole. He showed us how to hunt for gold. We panned for gold in Coker Creek, near Tellico Plains. We even found some flakes, maybe enough to buy dinner. He made toys and train whistles, and always wore a railroad cap.

The first time I met Joe Diehl was over at the Museum of Appalachia. John Rice Irwin was talking to this little old man beside a beat-up pick-up truck. They were trading, I think. In the bed of the old truck, that didn't look like it could make it across the street, lay this huge ancient millstone. There were ropes, an old wooden block and tackle, a come-a-long, and all this other stuff, some of which I'd never seen before.

After they were done trading, John Rice told me Joe had pulled this twelve-hundred-pound millstone out of a thirty-foot trench, down an embankment. He'd done it all by himself.

Years later, Joe was very ill. He wasn't expected to live much longer, but he was always smiling, calm, and soft spoken. We did a story with him where he made ink pens out of turkey quills and made children's whistles out of river cane. Joe Diehl always knew more than the rest of us.

I remember going to see Joe because it was a particularly difficult time in my life. I remember wanting to see him one last time because he always amazed you and taught you something about life and living. This day Joe was dying, there was no doubt. I remember exactly what he said to me that day. I'd asked him about life and the woods and the mountains and why he loved them so.

"Bill," he said, "you don't go to the woods to listen to the wind. You go to the woods to find the truth of things."

> *"You don't go to the woods to listen to the wind. You go to the woods to find the truth of things."*
> —Joe Diehl

Joe Diehl shows off some of his toys.

Museum of Appalachia.

Nature's Guides and Unlikely Explorers [45]

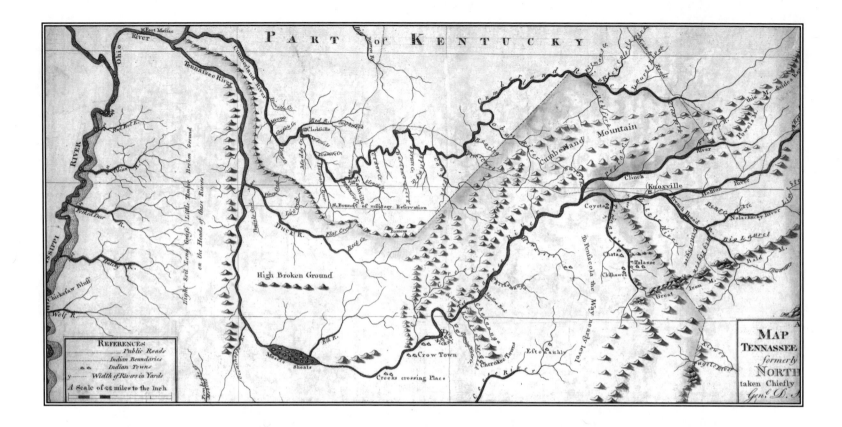

Map of Tennessee Government, formerly part of North Carolina, around 1796.

We Are All Unlikely Explorers

For William Bartram, Dr. Aaron Sharp, and for us, the forest is a wonderful place to teach and learn. The mountains and the woods are an excellent classroom with birds, trees, shrubs, trails, fish, insects, moss, lichens, reptiles, and more.

We learned that the Great Smoky Mountains National Park contains more species of trees than in all Europe, and more different kinds of plants than anywhere in the continental United States, except possibly the everglades. It has every conceivable kind of habitat in its half-a-million acres.

It's located in the middle of the Appalachian Trail between Tennessee and North Carolina, right smack in the middle of America. To botanists especially, the Great Smoky Mountains is heaven. It's a holy and spiritual place.

CHAPTER 6

April Fools

Viewer Support and Building Credibility

It was March 1987, the third year of the *Series*. We were sitting around asking the same question we always asked, "What the hell are we going to do next week?"

We'd been coming up with two new shows each week for three years now. We'd expanded the area of our focus by trying to do two stories in each of the thirty-three different counties in East Tennessee. This forced us to reach out to less familiar counties. We'd already met hundreds of key new folks from all walks of life.

They helped us by providing leads, story ideas, contacts, locations. They made calls to friends on our behalf. They found *Heartland* subjects for us. They invited us into their homes. We visited their farms. They allowed us to use their equipment and animals and develop bigger and better stories.

We continued doing stories with scientists, geologists, archeologists, and teachers. We pestered historians to death, calling to confirm information. It was a necessity. We had to be absolutely correct. If we weren't, boy did we hear about it in a hurry!

I once made the mistake in a voice-over of pronouncing the Appalachian Mountains with a long "A," as in the Appal-A-chian Mountains. The phone rang all week. I never did that again!

We realized if I was on camera, it had a certain ring of authority. The *Heartland* was saying this or that. But if Dr. Charles Faulkner, University of Tennessee Anthropology Department Professor of Archeology, was talking about three-thousand-year-old cave paintings, that's something else again.

Dr. Faulkner discovered the first petroglyphs in the region. He wrote a book on it, has a doctoral degree, and a great deal of credibility. Therefore, we learned if we let Dr. Faulkner say it instead of me, we would have more credibility.

The *Series* was reaching a broad audience with a lot of information. It was unlike anything else: environmentally conscious, conservation-based, unique, exact, true, and entertaining as well. We were beginning to understand and recognize our responsibility to make a difference in our community. We learned it from feedback and viewer's reactions. Jim Hart and Steve Dean knew it. Simply put, we might actually be able to improve the quality of life in our region and be of

Bird petroglyph, cave art.

Dr. Charles Faulkner at work, up to his ankles in artifacts.

real service to our audience. That's quite a responsibility.

We were working with botanists, historians, cultural resource people, folklorists, even musicians. We were doing stories on a wide variety of different art forms and sciences.

If we were doing a story on the Tellico River, or the valley of the Cherokees, we'd go see Dr. Jefferson Chapman at the McClung Museum. He wrote the book on Tellico archeology. Dr. Dave Etnier took us to Citico Creek and Abrams Creek, taught us about the fishes of Tennessee, and wrote perhaps the best book on freshwater fish species in the world. Wow!

Steve Ahlstedt identified mussels with us on the Clinch and Big South Fork Rivers. If we had a question, we'd call Steve. Dr. Jan Simek fascinated us with adventures in deep cave art, and Dr. Paul Parmalee educated us on prehistoric jaguars and the saber-toothed tiger artifacts he found near Chattanooga.

The Night of March 31st

They say that necessity is the mother of invention. I don't know who "they" are, but it might be the *Heartland* staff. Because that's how the April Fools stories came about. One March day in 1987, Sean, Laura, Doug, and I were talking about how our

Steve Ahlstedt at mussel habitat on Duck River.

audience was beginning to trust us. That's when someone said, "Hey, they're getting where they believe what we say. Let's just tell a big whopper." Then someone else said, "Yeah, like an April Fools joke!"

I remember as a kid reading Superman and Bat Man comic books every week when they came out. My brothers and I always looked forward to each new issue. One issue, particularly, stuck with me, "The Night of March 31st."

Even to this day, I love that title. In it things went crazy. Right was wrong, day was night. Superman couldn't fly! Everything was backwards. It was Bizarro World!

That was one of the ideas behind our April Fools stories. It was March 31st. We never said it was April Fools until the end. That would have given it away. It had to sneak up on you. You get sucked in a little at a time until you believe it.

So we started asking ourselves, "What does it look like?" TV is a visual medium—we have to see it—whatever "it" is. More importantly, "it" has to

April Fools [49]

"The night of March 31st. In it things went crazy. Right was wrong, day was night. Superman couldn't fly! Everything was backwards. It was Bizarro World!"

Steve Dean, WBIR Creative and Community Services Director. Our boss!

Doyle Dixon, WBIR's carpenter.

be something we can photograph. We pitched it to Steve. He liked the idea of an April Fools story and recalled seeing a video clip of the U.T. rowing team demonstrating how good they were by actually pulling a water skier up out of the water. You could see it, right there on the TV screen.

That's when we came up with the idea for the water skiing paleo-Indians. We used the actual video clip in the story, too. Most of our archeology stories involve prehistoric digs. So we thought, "All we have to do is dig a hole, run some string across it, and have some students there to work on the site." Presto, we had our own archeological expedition!

Steve Dean agreed to play the scientist, Dr. Don Masters ("Mastadon." Get it?) Dr. Masters was from Eastern Ohio State University which, of course, doesn't exist. We chose Ohio simply because we always had trouble driving in the Park behind tourons from Ohio.

The concept began to grow. The shoot required help. John Rice Irwin at the Museum of Appalachia let us use his farm on the Clinch River for the location of the fictitious archeological dig. The voice-over went something like this: "Today on *The Heartland Series,* we'll join Dr. Don Masters and his students from Eastern Ohio State University. They're here by the Clinch River working on a Ulysses S. Grant...."

I don't know anybody who has ever received a dime from a Ulysses S. Grant! Ha. It was early in the story. And even though that might have given it away, everything else looked and sounded like all our other archeology shows. The audience bought it because the program looked real enough.

Back at the TV station, the head carpenter—the only carpenter—Doyle Dixon was game for whatever zaniness we had going. The more excited we'd get, the more excited he'd get. Doyle is a kid at heart.

He took a couple of eight-foot pieces of two-inch PVC pipe, heated and bent them, and showed us how to shape them to look exactly like a pair of ancient water skis. We threw some coffee grains on them to color and age them, and tied some old leather to the skis. And, bingo! We had us a "gen-u-ine," prehistoric artifact, whipped out in Doyle's shop in two days for about ten bucks.

Back at the site, the shallow trench was dug, and we put the strings across it. Don Masters (Steve), says, "Come over here, Bill, and I'll show you what we've found, what we believe to be ancient water skis!"

We named the story "A Significant Find." Like all April Fools shows, this one was partly scripted. That is, some of the ideas, scenes, and gags were worked out in advance. But much of it was ad-libbed, made up as we went along. Steve was very good at ad-libbing. I would always play the straight man and ask the obvious questions. Then, I'd pretend to get mad at the end when I found out it was all a big hoax.

TVA Tellico archeology dig.

In these April Fools stories we could poke fun at ourselves. For instance, often on real shoots I'd ask Dr. Faulkner, "How old is that artifact, or arrowhead, or something?" And he'd say, "I don't know Bill. We'll have to go back to the lab and carbon date it and find out." It would always beg the question, "What the hell is carbon dating? How does it work?"

That's where the idea for the final scene came from. The water skis/artifacts are placed on two saw horses. Dr. Masters shows us what he has found. He says, "Don't touch that Bill, it's ten thousand years old!" Then, I ask him how he can be sure of the correct age of the artifact. That's when he pulls a piece of carbon paper from his pocket, places it on the artifact, and rubs it with his pencil. The camera zooms in for the tight shot.

Then, he removes the paper. Wow! There it is for the entire world to see: scientific proof writ-

Electric Trees

One of our favorite stories, and probably as good a joke as we ever pulled, is a show we refer to as "Electric Trees," although the actual name was "The Watt Experiment." Again, Steve plays the main character role of the scientist, Dr. A. C. Watt and says the usual goofy stuff. For instance, when I asked him if he was excited about getting energy from trees, Steve replies, "Sure. Frankly, Bill, we were shocked!"

As the show opens, we're at Norris Dam looking very small against the dam in the background. Dr. Watt muses maniacally, "Imagine Bill, if we could harness the volume of the mass of a tree."

He goes on to demonstrate his concept using a small digital clock. This idea comes from an actual fourth grade science experiment where two wires or diodes are stuck into an Idaho potato. It generates enough energy to turn the clock.

Dr. A. C. Watt continues, "Imagine if we could harness that energy from a tree!" We spend the rest of the show proving the hypothesis. We had a one-horse leaf blower hooked up to a 110-electrical socket hidden in the crook of a tree. When we turned on the blower, it blew the baseball cap off the technician's head, thus demonstrating the feasibility and practicality of this new scientific finding.

It's all shot and photographed on TVA's land where there's a multi-acre tree orchard below Norris Dam. We had footage of trees being planted and people putting stickers reading "110 volts" on the trees. The final shot was the coup-de-gras.

It's a wide shot of me alone. With trees in the background, I'm running a blender, mixing cold refreshments. I pour myself a drink and watch

Dr. David Etnier, Sam Venable, and yours truly at a dentist fishing contest!

ten on the ancient, bone-ski relic. It reads, "10,000 years old." It says so right there. That's when the gig is up. Steve, as Dr. Masters, claps his hands together and says, "Okay. That's it, gang. Let's pack up. We've got to get back to Ohio!"

Over the years, folks have told us they always enjoyed these April Fools stories and we looked forward to doing them. During the twenty-five years of the *Series,* we did, perhaps, twenty April Fools' Day stories. Two of them, in particular, are worth mentioning.

TV—Channel 10, of course. The camera begins to move, following all the electrical cords until it reveals all the cords are plugged in to one socket at the crook of a tree!

Meanwhile the voice-over narration closes the show. "They all laughed at the horseless carriage, too. But one day soon, electric trees will become a reality."

But the joke didn't end there! We forgot to put the words "Happy April Fools' Day" on the screen. We didn't actually forget. We didn't think it mattered. We'd been doing these April Fools shows for ten years. We thought people would realize by the end of this story that it was a joke. Well, they didn't!

I won't say people are dumb. But when it comes to believing what they see and hear on television— let's just say they are unusually gullible. It's funny now, but it wasn't too funny then.

When "The Watt Experiment" aired without the line "Happy April Fools' Day," Channel 10's phones started ringing. Without it, people thought the experiment was for real. It was like *War of the Worlds!* The phones rang off the wall. People believed in electric trees.

We even received a call from a Vice President of TVA wanting to know about this new development in electrical power. I answered the call and told her it was a joke. Well, she didn't think it was very funny! When I asked how she found out about it, she said she'd received a call from somebody at the Los Angeles Power and Light Company in California. She made me promise to call them, which I did. They didn't think it was funny either.

We received calls from community colleges. I won't say which ones. People were ready to run cables. One caller was so excited, he said, "I'm sure glad to hear about this new development in electric power generation. Hey! My backyard is full of trees!" He thought he was in high cotton.

Never again did we forget to put up the words wishing everybody a Happy April Fools' Day.

Elks or Elves?

While helping with the Friends of the Great Smoky Mountains National Park Telethon, one such idea for a good April Fools show presented itself. At the same time as the telethon was airing, the Park also was reintroducing an elk population into the Cataloochie area in North Carolina.

National Park spokesman, Bob Miller, told us about a call he'd received from a confused and irate taxpayer who was mad as a hornet about the use of American tax dollars to reintroduce *elf* into the National Park. Yeah, elves! He'd misread an article or heard something wrong. The caller thought the *K* was an *F* and elks were elves.

The guy went on and on about it. "Name one person who has ever seen a $@*& elf! No one, that's who! And where you gonna go to get you a pack of elves anyway? Tell me that, huh, if you could find you some!"

The more Bob talked and laughed, the more the wheels in our deranged little minds started to turn. Hee, hee, hee. This one had real possibilities. It was 2004. Amy Anderson had become the newest *Heartland* writer/producer. She came over from *Live At Five,* where she was producing. Linda Billman had left to produce *Trading Spaces,* which turned out to be a very successful show for HGTV.

Amy's sister happened to work at Seymour Elementary School. Amy contacted them to see if the first graders might be interested in playing elves on a *Heartland* TV April Fools story. You might as

"If the legend is better than the truth, print the legend."
—The Man Who Shot Liberty Valance

"A stawry, Bill, is always the truuuth. But it's a stawry."
—Ray Hicks

Frances Hudson, baby goat, and me.

well have asked them if they wanted to meet Santa Claus or have an ice cream party! You bet! They were in. So we had our elves. That was big.

While the first grade at Seymour spent the week making thirty elf costumes complete with little green, Spock-like ears, and tiny shoes that curled up at the toe, we rounded up other elements of the story. We borrowed a big, red cattle truck from Kim Delozier's father, who just happened to live in Seymour as well.

We contacted cabinet maker, friend, and musician Buddy Floyd to help us catch the elves. Buddy wore a beard and dressed in a kilt. He played the part of the greatest catcher of Wee People that Ireland had ever produced. Buddy looked great and concocted this fabulous story about being contacted in Ireland by an important man in the U.S. Government to see if he'd help catch the Wee People.

"They love music and dancing," the Great Catcher went on. "So at night, as I play music by the fire, the elves begin to dance closer and closer until suddenly I stop playing and reach out and catch them! That's how you do it!" It was a masterful performance.

We shot Buddy playing music at night by the campfire on his concertina and reaching into crevasses in the rocks looking for elves. We had wide shots of him in the rolling mountains of Ireland that looked suspiciously like the area around where Buddy lives in Knoxville.

Next, we asked TVA spokesperson and old friend Gil Francis to portray a government beaurocrat. His job was to explain how a *K* became an *F* in the proposal, and that it was funded anyway. Gil said emphatically, "The government stands behind this project one hundred percent. We're ready to move forward on it."

Finally, the big day of the shoot arrived. Mr. Delozier drove up in his enormous, red cattle truck with a huge sign that screamed, "ELF REIN-TRODUCTION." Doug got a great shot of the truck going by with the snow-covered mountains in the background. You couldn't miss the elf sign even if you were asleep.

The camera then cut to the large crowd which had gathered in anticipation, just like the real elk reintroduction scene we saw in Kentucky. They actually were the parents of all the first graders. They came out to help and waved signs that read:

"Welcome back Elves," and "You've been gone too long!" and "We love you, Elves!"

Amidst the shouts of "hoorah" stood the lone uniformed Park Ranger, Kim Delozier, bigger than life. In his official Park Ranger hat, he moved toward the truck. As he begins to open the gate, Kim, fights back tears of joy and puts his arm around my shoulder. With our backs to the camera, we're positioned any minute to see the elves run free.

The Ranger says, "Bill. I've been working all my life here in the Park for this day! I never thought I'd live to see it. (Sniff, sniff.) You know, it's nice to know they're out there, even if you never get to see them!" That last line's actually a line Don Todd first delivered about wolves and panthers in the Obed River Gorge in Morgan County eighteen years earlier.

Amidst screams and giggles, the cattle trailer door is finally flung open, and with the sudden force of a landing craft at Normandy, thirty-five elves hit the beach! Finally, the Wee People are set free! Elves are home again in the Smoky Mountains where they belong!

Turning cartwheels and laughing, they tumble out of the truck with joy and run across the hillside. You can see in the shot the snow-covered Great Smoky Mountains National Park behind them.

I remember one overweight little boy huffing and puffing, heading back to the truck for another shot, another take. He looked like any seasoned movie extra, quite proud of himself and the job he was doing, and rightly so. He looked up at me, smiling, knowing we were all in this together. I smiled back. He knew I was pleased and said, "Boy, it's hard work being an elf. Whew!"

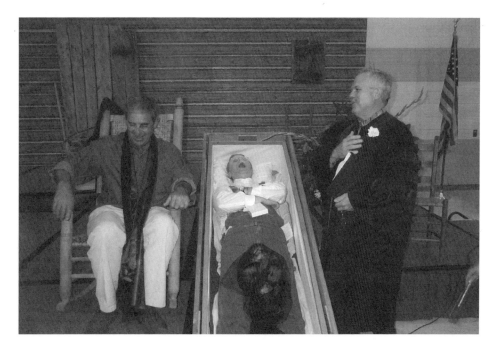

Usual suspects; Jimmy, Sam Venable, and me at the "Wake and Funeral of Jim Claborn." Note the non-decomposed body and the mouth that won't shut!

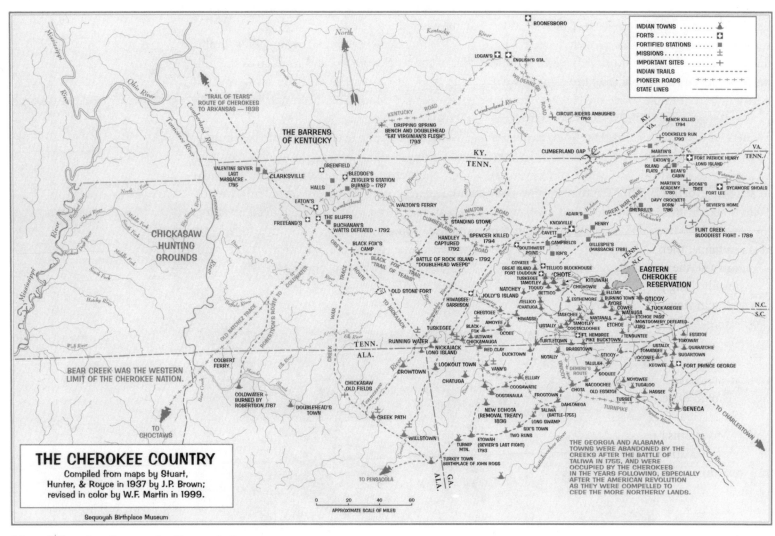

Map of Cherokee Country by George A. Reeves.

CHAPTER 7

Native Americans

My Brother, the Crow

Cherokee, North Carolina, is thirty miles from Gatlinburg, Tennessee. To find it from Knoxville, go east across the mountains to the top of the Appalachians, then down the other side on U.S. Highway 441, the road that runs through the Park.

The only thing you'll pass other than spectacular mountain views and photographic overlooks is Newfound Gap. Depending upon the traffic, it's a good hour or more from Sevierville.

Cherokee is a Native American town. It's on the Qualla Indian Reservation and isn't really part of the United States. The land is managed by the Cherokee Tribal Council and borders the Great Smoky Mountains National Park. Harrah's Casino, Oconaluftee Native America Village, the Cherokee Museum, and the beautiful Oconaluftee River await the visitor. Whatever you expect Cherokee, North Carolina to be, it won't be what you expected.

This day, we planned to meet Marie Junaluska at the top of the mountain. Marie is a member of the Tribal Council and a Cherokee translator. She was going to help us translate some opening thoughts for "We Endure—The Journey of the Cherokee." This is the 1994 special program we developed with Dr. Jefferson Chapman and his folks at the University of Tennessee and the McClung Museum.

Bill Archer and Doug had been shooting vistas and B-roll for the show. We were planning to record Marie's audio in Cherokee, but I couldn't remember where I was supposed to meet her.

As I've learned through all these years of *Heartlanding* and studying the myths and legends of the Cherokee, confusion is not always a bad thing. Through it comes enlightenment. That's a good thing, too, because I'm confused mighty often.

We waited for Marie. She was late. But I still wasn't sure if I was supposed to be at Clingmans Dome or Newfound Gap. Damn, I should listen more. Write stuff down. I hate being late. It makes me nervous and uncomfortable.

So, thinking we should be at Clingmans Dome, we drove there. That's when I found out for the first time, absolutely for sure, that the crow is my talisman, my brother. I had already known that in my heart, but I didn't know it in my mind, if you know what I mean.

What happened up there at Clingmans Dome, the highest point in the Great Smoky Mountains, was simple. As we sat there on the wall by the parking lot waiting for Marie, I finally became aware of

Native American woman pounding corn.

the crows, "caw," "caw," and making that clicking noise they make to each other. But this time I was absolutely positive they were doing their communicative hollering at me. At that moment when I looked up and realized this, the crows took off in flight, all of them straight back to Newfound Gap.

The message was crystal clear. There was no doubt in my mind they wanted me to follow them. They were taking me to Marie Junaluska who was waiting for us at Newfound Gap. It was just as clear to Doug. The animal world can communicate with our world if we're open to it.

I have a particular affinity to crows. As I write this at home in Happy Valley by Abrams Creek, next to the Great Smoky Mountains National Park, I can hear the crows bidding me good morning, as they do nearly every morning. They come off the nearest mountain to my trees by the woodshed and carry on. Just letting me know they are there, hoping we may have left them some bread. If I treat them well, they will continue to help me. Perhaps show me the way.

Later that day, as we were driving down the main street in Cherokee, Marie explained some basic Cherokee history, such as the seven clans. That seven is a sacred number. And she told me the story of "Unta Schooley," the Great Buzzard.

It was Unta Schooley's mighty wings that forced up the earth out of the mud and formed the mountains that became the Great Smoky Mountains that we know today.

It was James Mooney's great work, *The Myths and Legends of the Cherokee Nation* that helped me understand some of the myths of these people, their sacred potions, and beliefs.

As we drove down the street, I asked Marie if she knew the person who was going into the Medicine Man Shop, my favorite store. She said,

"Oh, that's Tom Underwood." There was a lineman working on a telephone line nearby and she knew him, too. Someone exited a shop and I asked her if she knew him.

"Yes," she said. "That's Johnny Mankiller. And over there's my cousin."

"That's amazing," I said. "You know just about everyone here, their parents and grandparents, cousins, and who their people are."

"You would too," she said, "if you lived in the same place forever!"

I've thought about that often. That's a long time—forever.

Before the First Tennesseans

Working with the East Tennessee History Center, I recall how successful the "First Families of Tennessee Project" was and how much it meant to so many people. Folks and their families received a diploma–like document. It was signed and sealed, officially. It was on a parchment-like paper and suitable for framing. It documented that their family dates back to the late eighteenth century and the settlement of this region.

Family names such as the Adairs, Beenes, Sullivans, Russells, Gregorys, Walkers, and Tiptons made up the bulk of the applicant requests and awards. These are the first sturdy East Tennesseans that came here to tame the frontier and settled more than two hundred years ago.

But Marie Junaluska just told me her family lived in the same place, not just for one or two hundred years, but forever. Think about that for a minute. I often tell people that even though we live only thirty miles away from these folks, the Cherokee are just about as much like us as we are to the Armenians!

A young Hayes Lossiah at Oconaluftee Village.

The Cherokee are a different people and have a different culture. They've their own country, for goodness sakes. It's the Qualla Boundary. If they want to buy or sell a piece of property or land, for instance, it must stay within the tribe.

We have done maybe forty stories, beginning with "The Trail of Tears," over our twenty-five years of *Heartlanding* and we've studied these amazing people since we began working on the *Series*. But sometimes I think I know less about the Cherokee now than I did when we started. William Bartram said they were the largest race of men he ever saw.

Oral Tradition of the Native Americans

Imagine a group of people that until one hundred and eighty years ago didn't have the written word. Everything had to be communicated orally through stories about life, family, dreams, love, everything.

"Grandfather, why is the sky blue? Where does the wind go when it blows? Where did the first fire come from? Why are crows black?" When these questions or others were asked, an elder or the Grandpa would say, "This is what the old people told me when I was a boy," and then he would proceed to tell the story about why the crow is black, how it got that way. The crow, you see, is the medicine bird. He can go where there's sickness and death and not be affected.

Imagine there were no books, hieroglyphics, Dead Sea scrolls, Code of Hammurabi, Magna Carta, printing presses, or Bibles. Nothing was ever written down. Everything you knew was experienced or handed down by stories and metaphors dealing with life.

The Native American world and the world view of the Native American are shaped by oral history. Much of their understanding comes from experiences that happened over two hundred years ago when many of the original myths, legends, and stories first were told about the long ago times, and at a time when the Native Americans regarded the land as their home.

Their homelands stretched far and wide and included three distinct and varied major groups: the Lower Settlements, the Middle Settlements, and the Overhill Settlements. It's only a third of those people that we refer to as the Overhill Cherokee. They lived along the Little Tennessee River Valley that today forms the southern boundary of the Great Smoky Mountains National Park. At one time, over forty thousand Cherokee inhabited the Appalachian Mountains of Western North Carolina and East Tennessee.

Now, imagine that most of the time this civilization had any contact or dealings with white people they were lied to or cheated! Their history of dealing with white people led not just to banishment, but to disease, genocide, death, and annihilation. It's not hard to understand why they are hesitant to get too close to us!

Tom Underwood and the Medicine Man Shop

The Medicine Man Shop in Cherokee is part museum, part craft store, and part art gallery. Every day before Tom Underwood opened the Shop, he went fly fishing in the Oconaluftee River.

The river runs behind the store and he always took his cats with him. He kept the trout he caught for dinner or gave a few to his friends. When he

Tom Underwood.

caught a sucker he just pitched it up on the bank for his cats.

Tom was the beloved co-owner and manager of the Medicine Man Shop for years until he died not too long ago. He'd been an Indian Agent and worked on behalf of the people for the government, just like his father before him. The Cherokee knew and trusted Tom, and Tom loved, trusted, and understood his people. For most of our twenty-five years, Tom Underwood introduced us, taught us, and helped us make the acquaintance of many wonderful Native American people.

He introduced us to William Lossiah, Amanda Swimmer, Hayes Lossiah, Walker Calhoun, and the great artist John Julius Wilnoty, just to name a few. Each had a deep impact on our interpretation and understanding of their world, as well as our own—the one we share together with them.

The Little People

I'm not sure where we first heard of the Little People. I knew it was in Cherokee, but for years I thought they were talking about the Irish leprechauns I grew up hearing about.

My mother was a Sullivan and I attended Catholic schools, so Irish songs and leprechauns were just part of my make-up. "I was born to it," as Effie Baker would say.

The Native Americans believed in the Little People, too. We met many folks who did. The Little People lived in the forest and played tricks on you or got you lost. Sometimes they would appear, stay awhile, and then leave again.

We were curious enough about this phenomenon to explore it. So on one trip to Cherokee, we set up an interview with a lady who told us about her four children playing outside by a picnic table. When she looked out the kitchen window she saw five children. She thought since the Little People live deep in the forest, a neighbor's child had come to play with her children.

Later that day the woman went outside to see the children, but only her four remained. She questioned them about the little girl they'd been playing with. "Oh," her children said, "she just came out of the woods, stayed and played, and then left."

They never saw her or heard from her again,

or from anybody who knew anything about her. The lady believed unequivocally that she was one of the Little People.

John Julius Wilnoty

The greatest soapstone carver and artist I've ever seen or met in my life is probably John Julius Wilnoty. His carvings of insects, animals, and ritualistic images are precise, spectacularly imaginative, and unique works of art.

I'm not sure if Wilnoty is able to work much nowadays because he suffers from an illness called narcolepsy, where he continuously falls asleep even while working. This happens often, and if he's working with knives, blades, scrapers, and cutting tools, it can be quite dangerous. I remember seeing his hands when we finally met him. They were covered in scars.

I would put his body of work up against any artist alive that I've seen. I love it, obviously. But it wasn't easy to interview him. That's when we first learned the meaning of Indian time.

In his shop, Tom Underwood had shown us examples of the art of John Julius Wilnoty. A few years later, after much prodding and many requests, Tom arranged for us to meet and talk with him, or at least we thought he did. We were to come over to Cherokee, spend the night, and meet the great artist himself, the next day.

We arrived about 9:00 or 9:30 a.m. Doug had gotten up at the crack of dawn and shot the sunrise in Cherokee. When we finally found John Julius's trailer where he lived with his wife and at least three or four children, after some difficulty explaining ourselves to his wife, it became clear he wasn't home.

It seems he'd risen early and gone up on the mountain to pick morel mushrooms. We asked if they were expecting us, but it didn't seem to register with her. "Well, we'll just come back."

I think we shot some B-roll of Oconaluftee River, ate some boiled peanuts, and killed time lying around on picnic tables. We came back right after lunch and still no John Julius Wilnoty. We messed around all afternoon too. Finally, it was nearly 4:00 o'clock and we still had the two and half hour drive back across the mountain. We thought we'd give it another try.

We knocked on the door of his trailer, waited, and to our surprise, he opened the door. We explained who we were and what we were doing, mentioned Tom Underwood's name, and told him over and over how much we loved his work. Reluctantly, he turned and said something to his wife and came outside.

He was a dark figure—in more ways than one. Over his shoulder we could see a little work area, a simple desk light reaching over a cluttered small work table in front of a soft, worn chair. Rough stones partially-worked, tiny pieces of sand paper and assorted carving tools lay scattered close. The entire work area might have been two and half feet

.John Julius Wilnoty.

Snake pipe and insect by John Julius Wilnoty.

with a shelf above it. There was no room in the trailer.

The first thing he said as he stepped outside was that he wasn't going to stay long. We quickly set up the gear and did the best we could, but he just wasn't interested in talking very much with us.

As I recall, he did let us grab a few wide shots, but that was it. What he did do was to take a piece of buckeye and with a pocket knife scrape off all the bark. It left these beautiful designs on the wood. He gave us each one and I kept mine for years.

John Julius reached into his pocket and pulled out a piece of soapstone he was working on and a little pistol, an actual gun. He smiled once briefly during our short time together. That was it.

We went back home. Later we returned and visited the museums where all of his works were on display. We shot as many of his pieces as we could find. Doug lit them well, and presented them as the beautiful works of art they are. We had an interview with Tom Underwood, one or two shots of John Julius, and just spent the rest of the show celebrating his great art.

It made for a great show because his art is so fantastic. It's probably the best way to have approached the story in the first place, show the art. So what if we didn't have much of the artist: a Native American, who was living on Indian time.

Mingo Falls and Stones that Bite

We heard about a magnificent waterfall from some of the Native Americans we met in Cherokee. It was the kind of local thing you didn't find on a map. That's the mission we were on this day.

In James Mooney's monumental work, *The Myths and Legends of the Cherokee,* we'd read about

Mingo Falls with unidentified woman on a bridge.

the great snake Uktana that lived at the mouth of the Oconaluftee River. That's where we were going.

It was down an unkempt gravel road. I'm not sure where it was or if I could ever find it again. When we arrived to where it looked like we could park our truck, there was a big sign that read Mingo Falls. The trail began just about at the sign.

When we took a closer look, right up next to the sign, we could see some writing. It was written or scraped into the sign with a knife of some kind. It was a simple, single statement. It read, "Death to the White Eyes."

We all looked at each other and assumed correctly that we weren't in Kansas anymore! We looked around and seeing no one, headed toward the falls.

For years on our excursions, Doug or I would pick up a memento to remind us where we'd been. We'd take it back to the office and put it into our Hall of Shame, a little three-shelved bookcase. It housed our trophies, relics, rocks, and junk. We had a bone from Daniel Boone State Park on which we'd written "Daniel Bone"; a piece of coal from two miles down the Blenheim coal mine in Kentucky; a corn cob from our "Gritted Bread" story; a piece of flint from the Hiawassee; and soapstone from Murphy that we found on a story/shoot with William Lossiah.

We were walking the quarter mile along the trail when I noticed it. It looked at first like a piece of flint. I walked up to it and immediately thought, maybe this IS sacred ground. I might better leave it alone and forget about taking something from here. But I bent over to pick it up and when I did, as soon as I touched it, it bit me!

I thought at first I'd actually been bitten by a snake. I'd picked up a perfectly simple little stone the size of a finger nail. There was nothing sharp on it. However, my finger was bleeding profusely, like a "stuck hog," as they say. I knew instantly we were on sacred ground.

I showed it to Doug. My finger almost needed stitches. We looked around and found nothing that looked remotely sharp that could have cut me. We got our shots and then got the hell out of there.

I told this tale, and told it for the truth I might add, a few times. It was one of those completely unexplained occurrences that baffled me. After a talk one time, a man in his late fifties or early sixties came up to me and told me he'd been to Mingo Falls, too. At least he tried to get there. He said he was using a map of some kind and was approaching the falls from just over the ridge.

It was marked clearly on the map he was using. He crossed the mountain and was lost, just like that. He crossed the other mountain and was still lost. He said he wandered all over the forest that day, absolutely convinced he was in the right place.

He said, "The headwaters of the Oconaluftee River are supposed to be right here! And each time I got closer, I was convinced I was in the right place. I wasn't." He said he never did get there. He never did find it.

I asked him what he thought about that rock biting me. Did he believe me? "Oh yeah," he said, "Absolutely, I've no doubt that you were bitten by a rock. I couldn't find an entire waterfall! I don't know where it went. I just got lost. I've never been lost." Then, he wandered off, scratching his head. I know we were on sacred ground.

The Blowgun Maker

Hayes Lossiah was a blowgun maker. Tom Underwood told us about him. He lived up Deep Creek. We traveled a long gravel drive to get up to his place. When we arrived, there was a fire burning in his front yard, and a fire in his kitchen, too. His curtains were burning while he was out tending the one in the yard.

The fire in the yard was for his blowgun making. The one in the kitchen was a grease fire caused by his skillet burning. We saw it as soon as we drove up and ran inside and put it out. It was a crazy way to start.

Hayes was an older man—maybe eighty when we met him. He didn't speak much English, but we were able to communicate with him. I often tell folks, I did an interview with a Cherokee who didn't understand a word I said. That was Hayes. He heard what he wanted to, though.

If you asked him something he'd bust into a giant, sweet smile. His great lined face would crinkle-up, and he'd hold a blowgun over his head and say: "This, what I do." "This, what I do!"

I often thought I should do that when people want to know about *The Heartland Series*. People who don't know the *Series,* or are not from here, will ask what we do.

I'll say, "We do feature stories about people. You know: quilters, a bear hunter, a Native American carver, or a trout fisherman. It runs three minutes and forty seconds, and features the people and the land of the region." They'll look at me like I'm speaking Arabic! That's when I think of Hayes and his reply.

I just want to hold up a *Heartland* DVD or tape, or the body of our work above my head, like Hayes, and say, "This is what I do." It would just be so much easier.

The fire in his front yard was to heat up an iron poker, to burn the center out of a six to twelve-foot long piece of river cane. When the poker gets white hot, he'll stick it through either end of the

Hayes Lossiah, the blowgun maker.

bamboo and singe or burn out the membranes. They are seals, a separator in the plant's yearly growth. If you take them out, you have a perfectly straight pole or rod.

You could run water through it, but if you're a blowgun maker, you make thistle darts to shoot through it, instead. It's excellent for use as a hunting tool and a weapon of sorts. Hayes's blowguns are about eight, ten, or even twelve feet long. The raw material, the cane, is abundant and found growing along the river banks on the Oconaluftee River. It also is used in making mats, baskets, and many other utilitarian items needed in the camps and villages.

For his darts, Hayes uses thistle gathered in the fall. He fluffs them out, and wraps them with a string, gently securing them to one end of the dart. The dart is made out of whittled hickory. It, too, is perfectly straight, maybe ten inches long, with the thistle on one end.

William Hebert, Two Bears, in full dress.

Hayes was a good shot with that blowgun, too. It pleased him greatly to make it for us and show us how to use it. He talked, also, about attending white man's schools in Cherokee that he was forced to attend when he was a boy. He said the Cherokee children weren't allowed to speak the Cherokee language at school. If they were caught speaking it, they'd get their mouths washed out with soap.

He described how terribly poor the Cherokee people were when he was growing up. They often ate only soup. That's why he started making blowguns, because they could be used to hunt small game; rabbits, squirrels, and birds. I asked him, "What kind of soups did you eat?"

He replied in that punctuated Cherokee cadence, "What kind of bird you got?" It was as simple as that.

Two Bears and Lossiah, the Myth Keeper

Next to Two Bears and his wonderful wife, Leslie, artist and carver William Lossiah was my favorite Cherokee friend. But first let me share about William Hebert. That was Two Bears' other name.

Two Bears is what William Hebert chose to call himself. It was his Indian name. The Bear, as we called him, was kind enough to bless my home, my cabin in Happy Valley, when it was completed. He did so, in the traditional way, by burning switch grass, offering tobacco, and praying to the four directions.

The Bear helped us often. My favorite Bear remembrance is about shooting an April Fools story on the marshmallows that grew in the spring. It was a pretty funny tale about marshmallows that grew on briars and got as big as pillows! Gary Farmer played the mallow hunter; Neal Denton gave us a scientific history lesson about it being Daniel Boone's favorite sweet treat. Boone called it, "America's Truffles." But in fact, it was a lot like baloney. In fact, it was baloney!

Anyway, the end of the show is one of my favorite all time shots. It's for sentimental reasons, as the Bear is no longer with us. It's a shot of Two Bears, who was along on that shoot. He was very sick then, and not able to do much, so we sat him down and built a fire in front of him. The Bear was dressed in traditional Native American dress, complete with jewelry and assorted trinkets.

The shot is from across the small fire, focused on him. He's seated cross-legged at the small fire, roasting something Indian. As the camera pulls back, still focusing on this hunter/warrior, it reveals what's at the end of the stick he's roasting in the fire. It's a marshmallow—that pioneer treat!

Two Bears was a great friend to me and the *Series*. We miss him.

The Myth Keeper

It was a beautiful fall day in Cherokee. We'd followed Tom Underwood's directions and found William out in his yard carving.

William wore a rough, old leather hat with a wide rim. He was a big man with a broad grin—perhaps, six foot three, and two hundred and thirty pounds. He laughed a lot, was friendly and outgoing. Later, William took us to near Murphy, North Carolina, to look for soapstone. That was when you could find it anywhere along mountain roads, by rocks and gullies.

William Lossiah was carving a big block of green soapstone, nearly two feet high and eight inches wide, a good-sized stone. He used a knife to carve it, and we watched and photographed him. Soapstone is easily worked with any blade and sandpaper. It's a very soft stone, but when polished is spectacularly shiny and beautiful.

William sanded, carved and talked to us about his work, the native traditions of his father, and his father's father, too. That's when he stopped working, looked up at us, and said in all seriousness, "I could write a book. But I can't write. So I make this stuff."

It made perfect sense. Making this stuff, his art, was his way of telling his story. His description of who he was and what he did for a living was echoed in his surroundings, his house, and many sheds. He was surrounded by his stuff, the raw materials of his many crafts—different woods, lumber, logs, stones, rocks, blades, sharpening tools, drawknives, etc.

His materials were scattered everywhere around his house and land, which was softly bordered by dark huge hemlocks that grew by the creek, the boundary. If William Lossiah wasn't an authentic Cherokee shaman or holy man, he was close to it, but he said the term was never used. "It's prideful to call oneself that," he said. I'd heard that before, too.

William's father was good friends with Swimmer, the great Cherokee Myth Keeper. Swimmer is one of the main sources of information in James Mooney's *The Myths and Legends of the Cherokee Nation*. Swimmer's picture is in the book.

The book is, perhaps, the most authentic collection of all the myths, legends, potions, and early Cherokee history. William said that Swimmer came and stayed at his house when he was a child. I think his family's connection to Swimmer is very exciting and interesting, and cool.

Before the turn of the century, maybe 1890, Mooney's book was commissioned by the Smithsonian Institution. They sent James Mooney to Cherokee to collect and document the old ways of the Cherokee before they were lost forever.

William was carving an old witch, Stonecoat. He told us the witch had a staff, and she would point the staff in the forest and smell the Cherokee people that way, find them, kill them, and eat them. There was another witch, too. He told us about Spearfinger. She was the original Freddie Kruger. She had a long, knife-like middle finger she kept hidden behind her back. When she got close enough to her prey by pretending to be an

William Lossiah.

"I could write a book. But I can't write. So I make this stuff."
—William Lossiah

Lossiah with art works.

"Everything," he said, "except love sickness! There's no cure for that!" Then he laughed and laughed.

William said at night when he would dream about something, an old story or tale from his father, the next day when he woke up he would make a mask or a carving or a sculpture of what he dreamed. If he didn't, the dream wouldn't go away.

That's the way he lived. He made beautiful masks carved out of balsa wood, or other materials. He told me how to make an Indian bow. He said, "Use yellow locust about four feet long and you carve it." But, I didn't have much luck with it.

I did take up carving soapstone and enjoyed it very much. Off and on, for about ten years, I'd go over to the Medicine Man Shop and get rocks, the raw soapstone. It comes in different sizes and colors, too. I even ordered some soapstone from a place in Miami, Florida, but the Medicine Man Shop in Cherokee, I found, is just about the only shop in this area where you can get soapstone.

I think I took up carving because of William Lossiah. He was a kind man and a good friend to me. He taught me a great deal. John Julius Wilnoty is a great artist and carver, but he was very eccentric and inaccessible. William helped me so much more and taught me much about the native people and their arts.

I just admire John Julius Wilnoty's work so much. He might be the greatest artist I've ever met or known—certainly one of them. His work is powerful, amazing, just astounding to me, mystifying. I love it.

But I can call William a friend. It's through him I've learned a little more of the mysteries and ways of the Cherokee.

old crone, she would surprise her poor victims, stick them in the chest, and tear out their heart.

William laughed about it, all these stories his father told him. He said there are stories and potions and cures for everything in Mooney's book.

CHAPTER 8

The Grips

Bill Archer, the Recordist, and the Position

This chapter is devoted to the unsung heroes: the men who fought in the trenches, walked through mud up to their knees, and in a word, actually two—carried stuff. These were the *Heartland* grips. They were actually the sound men as well. They were responsible for the audio.

Bill Archer was the *Heartland* soundman and he did that job exceptionally well for the last eighteen years. Actually, he was a recordist, which describes what the job entailed. He worked with Doug Mills. Recording good, clear audio was an important responsibility. It's one reason you remember the *Series* as a nature show. Bill Archer recorded most of it, and always did a wonderful, professional job.

Having a good sound man is mandatory if you want a quality show with good production values. Having a great sound person like Bill Archer was absolutely necessary for award-winning productions, the kind the *Series* consistently produced. We were one of the few production teams in local TV to employ a full time grip/soundman/recordist. I'll use the terms grip and recordist, interchangeably, for simplicity's sake.

During *Heartland*'s early years, 1984 through 1989, we didn't have a full-time soundman. Back then, we referred to our help as "a back," and they were part-time. What we needed at the beginning was help carrying stuff, "back work."

Traveling up mountain trails fifteen to twenty miles a week carrying television gear required strength, stamina, the ability to work with people; and the ability to be quiet. The sound man, after all, has to listen. When we didn't have a grip with us, usually the producer helped and ran the sound.

I'm not sure where the actual word *grip* comes from, but it probably has to do with grabbing. For that's what most grips do. They help with the set-up of the camera, lighting the shots, and helping move equipment, microphones, boom mics, batteries, etc.

The grip made sure the sound produced was clear, especially when working with musicians. That means no crackling sounds, or clothes brushing against sound devices. We usually interviewed people doing something, so it was important to monitor the sound for clothes rustling, which can ruin an interview. Also, for car noise, airplanes, boat motors, creek sounds, running and rushing water, etc.

Even with great video, if you don't have very

Bill Archer, WBIR recordist/soundman.

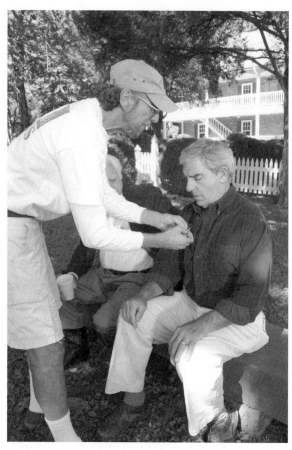

Bill Archer prepares John Rice Irwin and me for sound.

"Most grips hated going to get stuff. It was the demise of many an aspiring TV assistant."

good audio, you have nothing. We usually used two wireless mics and a boom mic when two or more people were talking. It was often hard to keep the microphones on the right people.

Here are a few stories about the grips we've gotten to work with over the years. How we attracted such good people to help us is a mystery.

The First Grip

One of our first and more colorful grips was a guy named Charlie. In 1984 when we began, after we'd hit the trails for a month or two, it became clear we needed physical help, and Charlie appeared to provide that help.

He was a Vietnam vet. He always wore an army jacket and talked a lot about fragging. Charlie could be a little scary. *Fragging* was a word used often in the military: a term for rolling a grenade under the tent of your own second lieutenant. So when Charlie would start talking about fragging, we'd scoot over to the other side of the truck, and give confused looks to each other. Charlie would just go on and on about his military reminiscences.

Bill Arant helped us often in the early days, too. He was young, handsome, athletic, and liked to catch "rays" when he got the chance, often on top of the *Heartland* truck at lunch while the rest of us relaxed in the shade. But if we forgot a battery or needed an extra tape, even if we were two miles from the truck, it never bothered Bill Arant to run a mile or two down a mountain and back again to get it. He liked it. Most grips hated going to get stuff. It was the demise of many an aspiring TV assistant.

Doug always took a little extra time at the truck, loading gear into packs, for if we forgot a battery for the mics, a tape, or batteries for the camera, or duct tape or anything, someone had to go back to the truck from Mt. LeConte or somewhere in the Obed River Gorge to get it!

It doesn't matter where we were, or what we were doing, even who we were with, for without a tape or a fifty cent battery we didn't shoot. We might as well not have shown up.

"First Man's Gotta Learn"

Occasionally, in the early days, Doug would say "We've only got one tape left. I've got to go back to the truck." If you do that a few times, you learn *not to forget*. But to his credit, Doug would always say, "No, I'll go get it. I forgot it."

"First man's gotta learn," is the way an old river man in Dungannon, Virginia, explained it to us once. An example of one of our worst experiences in forgetting something was on a shoot in Alabama about ancient bone remains found in a cave.

It was an archeological dig. We were with a group headed by Dr. Paul Parmalee, exploring remains of prehistoric animals. We hiked about a mile and a half, and then dropped over the bluff to the Tennessee River where we hiked another mile or more to the cave. When we got there, Doug realized we'd forgotten a tape. Yikes!

We could shoot a little while. We had one tape, but we had to send the grip back to get another one. This particular grip didn't want to go back! This grip didn't want the ball! He might have lasted another trip or two, but he'd had enough *Heartlanding* for his career. As it turned out, he later became a successful TV production vice-president or perhaps a banker, I don't remember which, but he did well.

One of the most grueling stories we ever worked on was probably "Downstream: From the Mountains to the Ocean." We were working on the first part of the story with Steve Moore, Park Fisheries Biologist, who for twenty-five years worked to restore the definitive Appalachian trout species. This required us to hike with him to brook trout land.

Now, brook trout, similar to black bear, don't live by the road, usually. They like high, clear, mountain streams, where you have to go to find them. We've documented the significant work of

Heartland ladies; Linda Billman, Laura Armour, and Alexis Magnotti.

Releasing brook trout.

Rangers and volunteers relocate brook trout.

Steve Moore identifying the subspecies of Appalachian brook trout. It often required scientists and rangers to remove rainbow trout from one place and return Appalachian brook trout to streams where they once existed.

On this particular trip we went way up Sams Creek in the Great Smoky Mountains to follow a drop of water from Clingmans Dome in the Great Smoky Mountains National Park to the Gulf of Mexico. It required us to follow its journey as it cycled through evaporation, from the mountains to the ocean, until it reappeared again as rain.

It was a wonderful show and won an Emmy Award. There's a great line from it that I'll always remember, "Nothing ever really goes away. It just goes downstream." It's clear, concise, true, and powerful.

But back to the story! The hub of TV work, at least for much of the *Heartland* team, was always the hard, physical work that outdoor shoots required. "Downstream" was sponsored by Southern Appalachian Man and the Biosphere (SAMAB), an umbrella organization made up of an alpha-

Steve Moore, Fisheries Biologist, has spent his career restoring native trout.

bet soup of federal and state organizations in our region: TVA, TWRA, EPA, Trout Unlimited, The Nature Conservancy, etc. It afforded us the budget to do the hiking and camping required on this shoot. The SAMAB project also allowed us the funds to hire Shaw, a Taos Indian, to help us.

Shaw—A Taos Native American

I'd met Shaw through some other people and knew he'd worked on movies, such as *Waterworld*, the Kevin Costner film shot in California. He was a movie grip—about six feet one inch tall, and weighed about two hundred pounds. But I've never seen anyone move through the forest like Shaw.

That's saying something, because we've worked with Elk folks, Rick Varner, Kim Delozier, and the hog hunter program to eradicate wild boar. These men spend a week at a time with a blanket in the wilds. This crew can hike all day chasing mountain animals and never break a sweat.

On this particular shoot we were going to the headwaters of the Little River where the story of "Downstream" opens. To get there, we crossed many streams—actually, many tributaries of the same stream. Up and up we climbed, carrying tents, TV gear, and food for two days. It was a camping trip and shoot. That's why God sent us Shaw.

A "man way" means there's "no way." Ha. I mean there's no trail. A man way is a place through the forest that a hiker makes. It isn't created by buffalo, raccoons, deer, or bear scampering up and down the mountain and then coming back the same way!

A man way is the way we climbed up to the trickling, bubbling, gurgling headwaters to shoot the wraps or stand-ups for "Downstream." We also did a lot of interviews. It was a beautiful location, but very difficult to reach.

We were about a mile below Clingmans Dome, but about six miles up by trail from Elkmont, carrying forty-five pounds of gear each. Doug was probably carrying more. I remember first seeing Shaw zipping around, up and down in the forest like a ghost; appearing from behind a tree, grabbing another pack and scampering up to our campsite. It was like he was part squirrel, a big squirrel. To watch him move in the woods was a thing of beauty, how he slipped instead of walked.

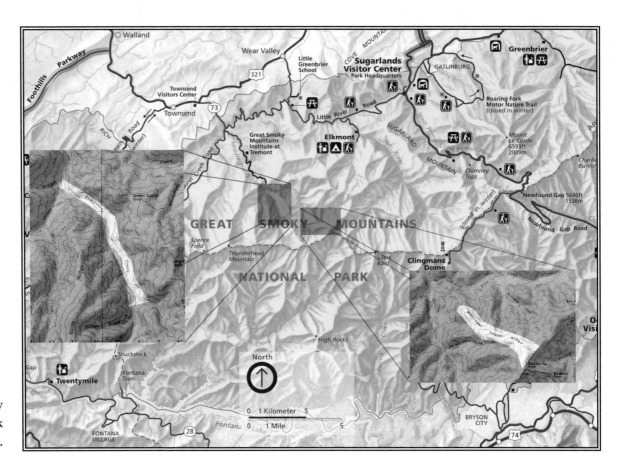

Map of the Great Smoky Mountains National Park showing Sams Creek.

We'd left the trail to make our way through the brush. Terrain was steep. He'd grab a sapling, step once, and was gone. You couldn't see where he went. He disappeared into the rhododendron and laurel. Shaw must have carried six packs by himself the last mile or so.

I saw him on his initial climb, just after he'd offered to carry another pack from an utterly exhausted biologist or *Heartland* member. He grabbed it by the straps, along with the seventy pounds he was already carrying, smiled, then zipped around like a squirrel up through the laurel, and he was gone.

Then, and this is the amazing part, he would return in ten or fifteen minutes, relieve Doug or me of our packs, and disappear again. He carried a hundred or more pounds, usually two full backpacks at a time to our remote campsite, and he did this two or three times.

When we finally crawled into the campsite, he wasn't even winded. He was making coffee. Shaw came from the Four Corners region where New Mexico, Utah, Colorado, and Arizona meet. His parents were close friends with the great artist Georgia O'Keeffe. His grandfather owned a huge ranch of thousands of acres where buffalo actually roamed free. Once a year, they were allowed to take a buffalo as part of a Native American ritual still practiced there.

He said, "We always took the buffalo as the old people had always done it, the old way."

We asked Shaw what "the old way" meant.

He said it wasn't with a bow and arrow on horseback. Their ritual involved watching the buffalo long enough to know its habits, where it was headed, where they were going. Then, you journeyed ahead and dug a shallow trench along the route, big enough so you could lay in it on your back and cover yourself to hide. Then, lie there and wait.

He continued to describe the ritual, saying, "We had two knives or short spears, one in each hand. When the buffalo finally stampeded across your slit trench, you simply thrust the spears into the belly of the two-thousand-pound animal moving very fast above you."

We were incredulous at this point. To say we stood there gawking with our mouths open would be an understatement. I'm not sure today if I truly believed him, but what he said next trumped everything.

Shaw smiled and held up his arms to show us the scars. He said, "They forgot to tell me to let go of the spears. I broke both my arms at the elbow. The buffalo dragged me. But, I didn't let go." I never saw Shaw again after that day.

John Davis, Bill Archer, Joanne Woods, Bill Arant, Andy Ramsey, Charlie, and many other hard working, fun folks worked as grips to help create the *Series*. On these long shoots there was plenty of time for tales and talk. The following is one of my favorite stories David Gowey told us. And he told it for the truth.

Gowey's Fifteen-Dollar Monkey Tale

David said he was in the Army Engineering Corp in the South Pacific or somewhere. They'd arrived on a jungle island to build an air strip. It was their second day. Upon their arrival, a local man, an entrepreneur in a small john boat, was already there.

He was selling Cokes, candy bars, and other snacks to the soldiers. They were doing a lot of hard work clearing jungle land with heavy equipment, and they took frequent breaks due to the heat.

During one of these, Gowey said the little man came over to them and brought a little monkey with him. The monkey was running up and down the man's arm, getting on his head and crossing his shoulders. As the monkey did this, the native man would hold him up and say: "Mon-key, monkey. Fie-dolla, fie dollar."

Gowey said to the man, "I don't want no five-dollar monkey. I want a fifteen-dollar monkey!"

Astonished, the little man said, "Fifteen-dollar monkey? Ooooo, fifteen-dollar monkey!"

"That's right," Gowey said to the man. "Fifteen-dollar monkey! I want a fifteen-dollar monkey."

They didn't see the man with the little monkey for the next few days. Then, sometime about four days later, they were at lunch when they were interrupted by a huge commotion. It was a horrible sound, like a monster growling. It was coming through the trees. Bamboo was being snapped and swished around, and small trees were falling down. Out of the jungle came four men, straining as they pulled on ropes.

Yanking and tugging for all they were worth, on the end of their ropes was this massive creature-thing. It was a big gorilla. Gowey said it looked like King Kong. It was a huge orangutan or gorilla-like thing, fighting and roaring as it was pulled by four native men in loin clothes.

"Gowey!" the Lieutenant screamed.

When Gowey talked to the native man and told him he couldn't keep that fifteen-dollar monkey, the little man broke down and cried. He'd probably spent three days hunting the thing with his brothers and uncles.

Gowey said he gave the man the fifteen dollars anyway, and told him he could keep the monkey, too. The guy was overjoyed and cried that he could probably feed his whole village for a week!

Gowey said he caught hell from the Lieutenant for this escapade. All Gowey could say in response was, "Gee, Lieutenant, I was just trying to buy a fifteen-dollar monkey."

CHAPTER 9

The Wit and Wisdom of the People

Jesse Holder and Mr. Cooper

Jesse Holder, a gun maker from Coker Creek, made wonderful handmade rifles. It was a thrill when he taught me how to sight one and shoot a finished piece. He always said, "I wished I could paint pictures from thought, but I can't. So I make these rifles to tell the story of the Old West."

Mr. Cooper, the millstone sharpener, lived up in Rennie, Tennessee, on the way to Jamestown on the Cumberland Plateau. He could take a giant millstone wheel and sharpen it by hand. To do our story with him, we spent nearly seven weeks trying to find a stone for him to sharpen. We couldn't take his mill apart or he'd be out of business.

Finally, we found a man in Kingston who had an old mill wheel. He loaded it in his pickup and drove it to Rennie, Tennessee. Doug set up the camera in Mr. Cooper's front yard. He came out in his overalls, walked over, took one look at the beat-up old mill wheel, and said, "I'd like to help you boys, but there ain't a thing in the world I can do fer that un." He turned around and went back to the house, leaving Doug and me with the truck, scratching our heads.

Mr. Cooper did sharpen that mill wheel for us anyway. The key is to chisel out the grooves without getting pieces of stone from the wheel in the flour and the meal. It's quite an art and was a service first performed by the Italian and Spanish stonemasons traveling this country a hundred years ago.

Using a hammer and chisel, Mr. Cooper went tap, tap, tap, cleaning fine little grooves in the stone. Doug moved around to get tight shots of the little flying particles. Finally, turning to me, Mr. Cooper said, "You ain't never seen nothin' like this before in your life have you, Bill?"

"No, sir," I said assuredly, and smiled.

"You know, Bill, there's a whole lot of things in this ole world that you don't know a thing about, ain't that right?"

"Yes sir," I said.

I never forgot Mr. Cooper and that saying. Shakespeare said something similar when Hamlet said to Horatio, "There are more things in heaven

1992 Heartland staff: Bill, Linda, Mr. Hart, Steve Dean, Bill Archer, and Doug.

and earth than are found in your philosophy, Horatio."

Mr. Cooper and Shakespeare are telling us something. I've tried not to forget it. There are a whole lot of things in this ole world that I don't know a thing about. Every day that proves truer than the next.

Knowing When to Take It to the Barn

I can't tell you exactly why "water witching" works, or why planting by signs works, or why folks cut boards so they won't curl up, only on the dark of the moon. These old ways are tried and true. They've withstood the test of time and they work just as day follows night, as surely as the sun rises and spring follows winter. But I can't tell you why and I don't think anyone else can either.

In Raccoon Valley, about a thirty minute drive from Knoxville, we were shooting a story on panthers, the eastern cougar, or "painters" is what the old mountain people called them. We'd interviewed some people who claimed to have seen a pair of mountain lions.

The mountain lion we were shooting this day was a pet. It wasn't actually trained, but would do whatever we tried to get it to do, almost. While we were working with this mountain lion, the man who owned the farm came nearly a quarter of a mile on foot to find us. He told us, in no uncertain terms, "You'd better leave!" Stunned, we asked why.

"The cows are headin' fer the barn," is all he said with a perfectly straight face, as if we were supposed to know what that meant. Finally, after a long awkward pause, he said, "Weather's coming in. You boys better start back to town while you can still make it."

He knew this and acted on it entirely because his cattle headed to the barn. We left right then. By the time we reached Channel 10, there was five inches of snow on the ground. The town was in turmoil, with cars crashing, people sliding down hills and through stop signs. Panic ruled. It was "get your bread and milk at all costs" time!

That mid-April snowstorm dropped nine inches of snow on us before morning. I made it home because that farmer came and warned us. But I did leave my Volkswagen bus stranded on Kingston Pike and walked the last mile home. It was so icy I kept falling down, but I got home before dark.

How people learn collectively and retain useful information has always fascinated us. I presume it's handed down in society to improve the quality of life. Traditions are learned, kept by the elders,

1935 riverboat landing below Market Street Bridge, Chattanooga.

Steamboat heading upstream. Note log rafts moored along bank.

we all thought. We'd adapt and build a smaller raft. The wood was green, too. Hmmm, that might lead to some surprises later, but no sense worrying about that now.

Week after week we returned to shoot the students' progress and thought we were nearing the conclusion. Everything was scheduled and ready. It was the day for the final send-off. We'd planned to shoot the twelve-by-eighteen-foot raft, completed and ready, and then head out and float downriver. Thirty folks had gathered at the farm where we built it.

Seriously and solemnly, family and students said a fervent prayer of thanks, prayed to keep us safe and sound on our journey downriver, and to please return us intact back home. We headed to the river bank where they'd tied the raft securely to a big tree. They'd finished it the night before. We couldn't spend the night there, but had come up early for the celebratory float. You can imagine the stupefied looks when we poked our heads through the thick brush that lined the bank and saw the raft sitting at the bottom of the river. Everyone was sure it would "swell" watertight in the water. Nope, it sunk instead! It didn't take long to figure out that, when it's built with green lumber, all it can do is sink. It wasn't dried. It couldn't swell.

No worries, we'll just have to make another six hour trip, back and forth. That's six hours travel, plus six hours for shooting, plus eating time. It was about this time in the history of the *Series* that we started to earn our moniker "The Heart Attack Series."

While all this was going on, we tried to find a first-hand source on flatboatin', someone whose family had earned their living in this way. We found him, too. He lived across the little lane from the river. This is what he told us about log rafting. "The old folks just knew when a big tide was coming, could tell by the sound of the river. Of course, there was no weatherman back then, they had to know. They were betting their livelihoods the raft wasn't going to end up stuck in some curve in a river bend. They'd float those rafts down to market, sell the goods, bust up the rafts, and sell the timber logs for lumber. Then, they'd walk back home."

The old man then took us into the dining room to a glass case and proudly showed us this beautiful hand cut glass vase. His grandfather carried that vase all the way from Chattanooga and gave it to his grandmother after one such trip. It wasn't broken or chipped and had been kept in his family for more than a hundred years.

Not satisfied with the information about the weather reporting, we asked him about the river and the tides it took to carry the rafts. Were there

Flatboat and log rafts. There are actually three rafts traveling together.

Flatboat and log rafts. Note the shelter aboard and the tiller for each width of logs.

floods? How many days rain for the river to rise and carry the rafts? Did it take two weeks to float to Chattanooga? How did people know when to go? That's when the ninety-year-old gentleman looked up at us and said, "First man's gotta learn."

With a barrel of tar and fifty pounds of sixteen-penny nails, the students went to work the following week to make the raft waterproof for the twenty-mile journey. Doug was prepared to shoot on board for half the run, if we could do it without getting the camera wet. But, we needed shots that captured what it was like to race down a swollen river aboard a log raft. We wanted to see

The Wit and Wisdom of the People   [83]

Lucinda Oakley Ogle at her cabin.

someone lean into that tiller, and get sprayed by water rushing by!

The raft was finally, *finally*, all nailed shut, tight as Dick's hatband. The tide was beginning to rise. Everything was set and we returned to see the old river man once more. We found him sitting under a tree in his shaded yard. He smiled when he saw us all heading toward him, the entire crew of about twelve men and women, mostly students.

We introduced ourselves as the crew of the flatboat. We all had feathers in our assorted caps. One student's research found that whoever captained usually steered the craft and drove the tiller. He was usually the toughest man in a fight, and there were plenty of fights in rafting days. The captain wore the red feather. The term "show the feather" comes from this tradition, meaning to run as from a fight. For instance, "He sure showed the feather that time!"

We thanked the old river man and invited him along. He actually considered it for a moment. Then, looking around carefully at the crew and with a twinkle in his eye, he shook his head and said, "Ha! If I'm going, I'm steering!"

Lucinda

Lucinda was one of a kind. I never heard anyone ever refer to her using any other name. No need. There was never any question who you were referring to, like Madonna or Mother Teresa.

Lucinda Oakley Ogle was the oldest daughter of Wiley Oakley. Dr. Aaron "Jack" Sharp introduced me to her when *The Heartland Series* was still in the idea stage. The significance is that Lucinda was the first real mountain person I met, and Dr. Sharp wanted me to meet her because he knew she was special.

Lucinda was both a daughter and queen of the Smoky Mountains. The mountains were the main source of her strength. She had an enviable sense of child-like wonder about life. I'd say Wiley, her dad, instilled that in her.

After even the briefest time spent in her presence, any flatlander would instantly gain a greater understanding of the language, customs, life ways, folklore, heritage, and traditions of the mountains.

That became her purpose in life, simply to share her love of the Great Smokies with anybody who would listen.

That little cabin of hers was probably the birthplace for the human aspect of *The Heartland Series*. During my first meeting with her, she showed me a record her dad Wiley had made with two of his favorite tales on it. Amazingly, she just gave it to me. It contained the tales "How Wiley Caught the Bear" and "The Cow Barn."

It was the first time I'd heard the true lyrical wonder of mountaineer speech. I shared it with the crew at the station. Excitedly, we put it on the turn table and heard Wiley Oakley say, "That's a mighty few werds to leave that gurl up here in these wiild mountains! Up hyere among the bears, and the bobcats, and so-on. Mabe better see her out!"

It was thrilling. It opened a new world to us. Little did we know it would become our twenty-five-year mission, our life's work, I guess. We were so excited to hear the real thing, an authentic mountain storyteller, and the best: Wiley Oakley. He was alive and we were in his presence.

Lucinda opened the door for us with that recording. A physical artifact connected us through technology to a different time and place. It was Steve's idea to let Wiley tell his own story. It became a way to work: let the people tell their own story. So, we shortened the tale a mite, and in 1984 produced "The Cow Barn," a reenactment tale.

Lucinda was a botanist as well and spent endless hours in support of the Smoky Mountain Wildflower Pilgrimage and the Gatlinburg Garden Club. Like Herb Clabo and a few others, she had a great need and spirit to communicate the beauty and the wonder of the Great Smokies. If Wiley introduced the Great Smoky Mountains to the world, Lucinda helped us to understand it, and more importantly, understand the people who inhabited it. She loved life and loved to pass on her rich heritage to those who took time to listen. Like Glenn Cardwell says, "Nature, history, and heritage were her loves."

Lucinda Oakely Ogle as a young student on her way to the Pi Beta Phi Settlement School in Gatlinburg.

The Wit and Wisdom of the People [85]

Linda Billman producing a story.

Linda Billman

I've been thinking a great deal about Linda Billman in anticipation of telling you about her contribution. Without it, much of what is *The Heartland Series* would not have been.

She's a part of nearly every story and episode from 1988 through 2000. Her personality and imprint is on nearly eight hundred episodes of *The Heartland Series*. As the writer and producer, she directly impacted almost half of the *Series*, an enormous amount of work.

Linda started in radio at WRJZ in Knoxville when C.P. & Walker was the highest-rated radio show in the market. Steve Dean hired her in 1988, the fourth season of the *Series*, to be our producer.

The Heartland Series was hard on writers. It was a good job, but a tough one. It was a grind, a merry-go-round you couldn't get off; always another show to write, one to shoot, and one to shot sheet, which was the boring part of the work.

Shot sheeting required the writer to sit with a video tape player for hours at a time, transcribing what was said from tape. The writer's job, basically, was to pick the sound bites, then write the script. It was the backbone of the show. We spent hundreds, thousands of hours doing this. During her time with the *Series,* Linda did more than her share.

It might take three hours to shot sheet a tape. It did me. Often there were five tapes. That meant fifteen hours' work before a word was written. The year before Steve hired Linda, we produced forty-eight episodes and a thirty-minute feature without a writer/producer. That meant Doug, Steve, or I, or some combination, found the stories, shot the stories, and wrote the scripts. In addition, Doug did "Straight from the Heart" promotions, while I spoke to various groups and found stories. It was almost too much for us.

Linda arrived to breathe new life into the *Series* and elevate it in stature and quality. She was fast, too, and really served as Assistant Executive Producer, until around 2002 when she left.

An excellent singer, she sings in a professional group, LB and the Radons, and understands the music of the region better than any of us. An avid hiker and conservationist, she serves on many environmental and conservation organization's boards of directors. Linda is currently General Manager of WDVX, the bluegrass radio station that began in a camper and is now heard around the world. She has come just about full circle, back to radio where she got her start. She's doing for WDVX what she did for *The Heartland Series* at a time when we needed a jump start.

I respect Linda Billman more than just about

anyone I've ever worked with, and now that the *Series* is over, I find myself realizing more and more how much she contributed to its success. I can still see her on the bat shoot—working on a story called "Bats on the Wing!" There was a close-up of Linda, smiling, but she was in trouble!

We were in a mine and had put on waders, but were one pair short. Linda didn't have a pair. Now, I don't think I'm being offensive if I say Linda isn't tall. I think she'd agree. She's an adult. The fact is she may be five feet and four inches tall, if she stands on a pile of phone books.

"There's some water in the mine," is what I thought we were told. They didn't say the entrance to the mine was flooded. Linda was sloshing around; about to go under with water up to her armpits, when suddenly, whoosh! She was swept up and saved by the big strong arms of an Adonis-like, park ranger. It was Kim Delozier to the rescue! He was always the gentleman, too. Linda always turned beet red when embarrassed. Well, she was beet red that day when Kim grabbed her.

A "Painter" Sighting on Eagle Creek

This is the story of the shoot where Linda, Doug, Bill Archer, and I got our first solid, "I swear on a stack of Bibles" look at an honest to goodness panther up Eagle Creek.

Park rangers Kim Delozier, Bill Stivers, and Rick Varner were researching the threatened brown bat populations in and around caves in the Park. The wildlife rangers had planned to carry a jeep by pontoon boat across Fontana Lake in the winter when the lake was down.

The pontoon boat came from Fontana Village Marina. It's a two-hour journey from Knoxville via Highway 129, called "the dragon" because it has more than three hundred curves. Fontana Lake was down thirty-five to fifty feet below normal for repairs to the dam. The jeep was necessary. Without it, the distance was just too far to hike in one day: two or three miles across the lake, another mile and a half along the lake to the trail head, and another five wilderness miles to the mine.

Arriving across the lake, they unloaded the jeep, and drove up Eagle Creek watershed to the old copper mines where the bat population had taken roost. We arranged to go with them to document it. The old copper mines were deserted, and bats had been using the mines for decades. A deserted mine is an ideal home for a brown bat. It

At the foot of Bullhead, Doug Mills and Linda Billman strike an American Gothic pose.

On a farm in Rockwood, Doug gets a moving shot from Roscoe Stinnett's jeep.

serves as an unusually good incubator where bats can breed, raise their young, and continue their cycle of life.

Even in a jeep, traveling a mountain trail up Hazel Creek or Eagle Creek, whichever the hell trail we were on was hard going. There were seven of us in the jeep, but it sure beat walking.

Of all the journeys and adventures we've had into the heart of the half-million acres that make up the Great Smoky Mountains National Park, this particular trip was as remote as we've ever journeyed. In fact, it was on the exact trail traveled by Horace Kephart, the trail he described as the "back of beyond" in his book, *Southern Highlanders*.

We were driving along, returning from the mines to the shore, bouncing from one rutted-out hole into another, along the rocky trail. It was like driving in a ditch. The trail was below, the wild lands above it. It wasn't a creek bed, though. The trail had been worn into the earth over hundreds of years by horse and wagon traffic, people and animals.

Suddenly, a mile or two from the mine, as we talked and bounced up and down, certainly not looking forward to the ride down the dragon, we saw a panther. It appeared quickly, coming out of the laurel and rhododendron thicket on our left. It bounded in the center of the trail in front and leapt into the thicket on the right. The trail couldn't have been six or eight feet wide. The panther, without exerting itself, simply sprang into the middle of the trail and loped on.

There's no question what it was. It was a panther, a "painter," as the mountain people say, an eastern cougar, a mountain lion! Its fur was brown, tawny, with a large flowing tail that looked to be four to six feet in length. The animal's body was maybe four or five feet long. It might have weighed ninety to a hundred-and-twenty pounds.

I was in the front riding "shotgun" and might have gotten the best look at it. First, we thought bear, but it wasn't a bear. It was light brown. Too big for a bobcat and it wasn't a coyote; its huge tail gave it away. We stopped and checked for tracks, but couldn't find any, and went home. It's the only wild panther I've ever seen in the Smokies.

• • •

WE ALL CARED A GREAT DEAL about the stories, these shows, and each episode. Occasionally there would be some conflict and disagreement, but we all respected and trusted one another enough to have our say, and let the chips fall where they may.

Linda was book smart, and relied on research and facts. I was more intuitive. I trusted the people who told me things, colloquial information, and folklore. Often, that put Linda and I at odds on things. Doug's point of view was objective and gave us balance. We usually accepted Doug's verdict.

For years, we did this. We were lucky. I was lucky. I finally began to learn that this thing wasn't my entire responsibility. I didn't have to carry the load. Linda and Doug were there to help if I would just let them.

Doug's Coal Mine Cave-In

Doug is from Kitts, Kentucky, near Harlan and his father was a coal miner. Doug would set up, produce, and usually write the coal mine stories. He knew more about that subject than any of us.

"Way down in a coal mine, way down in the bottom of a mine . . ." I remember those words from the first coal mine story we did, "Working in Coal." It was the only time I saw an actual cave-in taking place right on camera. And Doug would've gotten more footage except the guy holding his light took off running and left him in the dark with the camera rolling. That guy was me! It's a good thing, too, because Doug would've stayed down there shooting until the roof caved in and the whole mountain fell on his head. He was stubborn like that.

Doug had arranged with someone he went to school with that we would be allowed to go two miles underground to shoot this coal mine episode. Doug told me recently that the mine was the Blenheim Mine and was owned at the time by United Harvester. It was a day in the life of a coal miner kind of story. I'm not sure if OSHA rules allowed it or not. But we found ourselves dressed in jumpsuits as miners, with hard hats and lights, and traveled in with all our TV gear.

The miners were removing huge sixteen-foot

Doug Mills during the full beard phase, grabbing nature shots in field of flowers.

square blocks of coal from a large underground cavern that stretched hundreds of yards back into the darkness. In doing that, they stuck thick white oak timbers, maybe five feet in length, every ten or fifteen feet throughout the area to hold up the roof of the mine. Thus, the words from the old song, "Big Bad John": "Then came a day at the bottom of a mine, when a timber cracked and men started cryin'. . . ." Well, men didn't cry that day, except for me, but we sure heard the timbers crack!

Linda, Doug, and I—I don't think Bill Archer went with us—were two miles down in the dark-

Two spelunkers.

I was holding the light, bent over like everybody else. Doug, of course, was shooting. We recorded a miner going in front of the camera and saying, "She's getting ripe," meaning the mine. Then, all hell broke loose.

More specifically, the world rumbled and the roof caved in. That's when you could hear a miner's voice caught on camera, along with a lot of other crashing, rumbling, screaming, and shouting noises, "Run, goddamn it, run!" I didn't wait to be told again! My light and I were *not* the last ones out of there: Doug was! That's why people will always remember *The Heartland Series*. Because of work like that in the coal mine by videographer Douglas D. Mills.

After the smoke cleared and real coal dust settled, and the guy with the light finally returned to where the cameraman was, we hooked the equipment back up and saw the two-hundred-yard room was now a thirty-five-yard room back into the darkness.

That show "Working in Coal" is special. It's made even more so by this amazing piece of video. I doubt anyone who reads this, and didn't get to see it, will ever have a chance to see what an actual coal mine cave-in looks like. That's one scene that probably will never be shot again, by anybody.

ness. The ceilings were about five feet tall so miners walked bent over with their hands behind their backs to help keep their balance. Everyone was getting pretty nervous, and with good reason. The earth was making noises, rumblings. The timbers were under great strain as the earth inched ever so slightly down, down. Hard hickory and white oak began to pop. Right then, it started! It's the only time you can hear profanity in a *Heartland* episode, if you listen carefully.

Most of the coal had been removed from the section they were working on that day. Miners actually do "jam" those timbers in the four or five foot seam of coal when they remove the pillars that hold the roof up. They actually try to make it fall, i.e. cave-in the roof, for once the coal has been removed the mine isn't safe until the roof falls. Hell of a way to make a living, huh?

Working a Twenty-Seven-Inch Coal Seam

Fifteen to eighteen years later, an older, but I don't know how much wiser, *Heartland* crew went into another mine in Campbell County, Tennessee. It was a family mine, and coincidentally, that's the title of the story—"The Family Mine."

The Campbell family worked a small truck mine. A truck mine is simply one where the coal that's dug is transported by trucks and sold. It's usually dug, sold and transported all by a small family or group. Their mine wasn't big either, but by working hard they could earn a living working in a twenty-seven-inch seam of coal.

Now think about that. Twenty-seven inches is a tiny bit larger than two feet. And you know how short that is. Imagine working all day, every day, on your side with a shovel and/or a pick axe working coal in a twenty-seven-inch seam. That means the roof is twenty-seven inches from the ground. That's not much room.

"The Family Mine" was also an interesting coal story, and it was an amazing day shooting in that mine. We traveled down into where they were working in the scoop of a *miner*. A miner is what they call the big machine that actually scoops up loose coal. The machine is perhaps seven feet wide, but very short. It's no more than two feet high, with a long, wide, short scoop on the front of it. We were able to lie in the scoop and be hauled miles into the earth with the ceiling passing inches from our face. We traveled at four or five miles an hour moving through darkness except for the light from our miners' hats! It was quite a day and a wonderful story.

When they shoot off dynamite to blast a section loose, it sends wind and a shock wave throughout the mine. And they do yell "Fire in the hole!" before they blast it. Linda went with us, and I was near her when they shot off the dynamite. It was like "G" forces let loose. Our faces, our cheeks sort of fluttered with the percussion, as the wind blew by us. Then, everything went back to normal—if living your working day on your side in a twenty-seven-inch seam of coal is normal.

Our grip for this story, Bill Archer, swore that he would never do it again. "Never, ever, go down in a coal mine again!" And he wasn't kidding. It was . . . different.

Doug's Work—
What a Picture Is Worth

When you consider the number of episodes that *The Heartland Series* produced, it's an amazing body of work. Consider the number of camera shots taken to create nineteen hundred episodes. Now realize only one person took nearly all that footage: Douglas D. Mills, the *Heartland* videographer.

Rod Kirby began the *Series,* and shot nearly everything in 1984, our first year. Then, Steve Dean told Doug that he was going to be the videographer and almost everything seen in the *Series* from 1985 until the last episode was shot by Douglas D. Mills.

Usually, if Doug wasn't available, it didn't get shot. We didn't want to use anything in the *Series,* if Doug Mills didn't shoot it. That's an amazing compliment to the man and his craft. Black bears, wolves, darters, trout, snakes,—and Doug Mills hates snakes!—snakes copulating, water snakes fishing, Peregrine falcons soaring—these animals don't pose for the camera!

Somebody had to get up at 3:00 or 4:00 a.m. to get atop Clingmans Dome to get that sunrise over the mountains, or to get in a wildlife blind in Sweetwater to shoot those sandhill cranes arriving in a corn field. That stuff didn't just happen magically. It took hours and hours of hard work, discipline, travel, luck, and experience. And through it all, I never heard Doug Mills complain about it, except once.

Doug washes cable in winter.

The Wit and Wisdom of the People [91]

Elmer Sherwood, the board splitter, at John Rice Irwin's Museum of Appalachia.

As Gus said about Deets in *Lonesome Dove*, "He never shirked a task. Cheerful in all weathers, splendid behavior." Doug never missed an engagement, and was there serving with distinction at all times.

Intro to the Aquacam

One more note about our gear and the inventiveness of "Danger" Mills. When we traveled down the Holston, French Broad, Tellico, Ocoee, Nantahala, Big South Fork Rivers; or climbed Mount LeConte (five times), Mount Mitchell, Roane Mountain, Spence Field, Thunderhead, Rocky Top, Clingmans Dome, Gregory's Bald, Andrews Bald; or when we went to Coldetz Cove, Cumberland Falls, Dale Hollow, Norris Lake, Watts Bar, Chattanooga, Manteo and Kill Devil Hills (NC), Utah, Reelfoot Lake, La Fete and New Orleans (LA), we always carried all that gear with us.

Today, video crews use a digital camera that weighs about four pounds with everything included. It shoots beautiful H.D. (high definition) pictures/video on a computer chip the size of less than your fingernail. It's about half as thick as a credit card. Most of *The Heartland Series* video was shot using fairly old school equipment, though it was the best of its day. We just did stuff the hard way, until we could figure out an easier way to do it.

Doug invented the Aquacam, and this gave us a leg up on the competition in underwater photography. It's the latest thing in underwater photographic equipment. It works like this: go down to K Mart and buy a twenty-dollar aquarium, take it to Little River, Abrams Creek, or Citico, wherever you need to shoot underwater, and sink it. Place your camera inside the aquarium and hold on to it. Push down hard on the outside frame, but not too hard. Don't get any water inside the aquarium. It's amazing how good and clear the video is. It's excellent. Occasionally, Doug may have to wipe the moisture off the glass or dry it, but it works amazingly well. He invented this technique and has gotten beautiful underwater footage for years using it. He's shot brook trout, darters, snails, sauger, and crawfish in it.

Doing two shows a week, it wasn't uncommon for us to hike fifteen to twenty miles a week, dragging that gear, week in and week out. We both weighed about one hundred and eighty-five pounds when we first started in 1984. By Christmas that first season, after the first fifty-two episodes were shot, I weighed one hundred and sixty-five pounds. It was a physical job for all of us.

Plate 1. Clouds over mountain.

Plate 2. Mist on Little River.

Plate 3. Walter and A.D. Bohanon and me, fishing the Little River.

Plate 4. Peregrine falcon in flight.

Plate 5. Mature red wolf.

Plate 6. Copperhead.

Plate 7. Mingo Falls.

Plate 8. Otter in the Little River.

Plate 9. Rhododendron in bloom.

Plate 10. Dolly Parton and me.

Plate 11. Solo Caver.

Plate 12.
Devilstep Hollow Cave.
(Marion O. Smith).

Plate 13. Sunlight through trees.

CHAPTER 10

Stories, Tales, and Storytellers

Wiley Oakley—The Roamin' Man of the Mountains

Wiley Oakley is the famous mountain guide and storyteller who called himself, "the roamin' man of the mountains." He was born at the foot of Scratch Britches Mountain, and he said it took him eight years to get to the top!

He was the first guy in Gatlinburg to put out a sign on the old Gatlinburg dirt highway that said, "Antiques—Made to Order!" He once found the skeleton of a man caught in a bear trap.

Nearly twenty years after we first heard this, it turned out that the skeleton Wiley actually found was the remains of Jasper Mellinger, another person we feature in this book. So, you see, many of the tales and stories of the mountains are interwoven.

From the beginning, Wiley Oakley meant a great deal to us in the *Series,* and to me in particular. He was a performer and storyteller. He played a little music, but primarily he was a mountain guide.

It was Wiley who introduced and helped convince the senators and congressmen to include the Smoky Mountains along with the Blue Ridge Mountains of Western North Carolina in the proposed National Park.

Wiley took a great many politicians to LeConte to see the Tennessee side of the Great Smoky Mountains. His gentle nature, stories, and subtle mountain ways charmed them enough for the Tennessee side of the Smoky Mountains to be included in the newest National Park.

Early in planning *The Heartland Series,* we weren't sure if I was going to play the character of Wiley Oakley, as the host of the Series. If you watch the pilot episode, "William Bartram, the Flower Hunter," you can hear a slight feigned twang of a mountain accent. Over time it became clearer. But, at the beginning, at least, I had Wiley Oakley fever. Lucinda had given me an old 45-rpm record with "The Cow Barn" on one side, and "How to Catch a Bear" on the other. We listened to it often to hear firsthand that unique southern mountain dialect.

The character came to life with the help of that record, and we used the recording as the script for

Wiley poses in front of the Wiley Shop, his store.

"The Cow Barn," with Wiley himself narrating. It was our first great story and perhaps the best episode of our first year. Later, we used two more of his stories as episodes. Wiley Oakley's "The Sheep Eye" and "Wiley's Dog Gone," both required actors and were a lot of fun. It was an honor to have the real Wiley Oakley telling a story.

His humor, understanding, and love of the mountains and its people are evident. His books *Roamin'* and *Restin'* form the foundation of our understanding the people of this place.

I was told the following Wiley Oakley story by two different people. Both heard Wiley telling it on the street in Gatlinburg while he was hustling a tour group to take to the mountains. It's the way he made his living.

When he had a group together, he'd charge them a small amount and take them on a hike. He would introduce them to the plants, animals, and folklore of the mountains by telling tales along the way.

At dinner time, so the story goes, he'd stop at the foot of an old balsam tree, explain that it was a female fir tree, and she had the fruit. The male tree didn't. Then, he'd start digging, and come up with a passel of Irish potatoes he'd planted previously.

The audience of Yankees and flatlanders were suitably amazed. Amidst "Ooos and Ahs" they shook their heads in awe of "a real mountain man!" Wiley cooked up the taters and made a big meal for everybody. His sole purpose, of course, was to get a nice tip, which he often did.

"Layin' out of a Night," is one such tale Wiley told. When he finished telling a tale and yodeled, that meant you might not take it "fer the truth." It's just a tall-tale. But if he didn't yodel, it was told for the truth.

[94]   Appalachian Tales & Heartland Adventures

"Layin' Out of a Night"

"I was out a huntin' one time of a night, had gone way up past the cow barn into the high mountains. I had my powder horn, my pouch, and my rifle gun. I got caught out with night coming on, and it got dark.

"Well, weren't nuthin' fer me to do but to lay out of a night. So, I found this big fir tree, balsam, and laid my powder horn and my pouch up on this limb. Well, directly here comes that ole moon up. Might a been a new moon, don't rightly know. But, that old moon come up and picked my powder horn and my pouch clean off that limb and carried it plumb across the sky!

"The next day I couldn't hunt 'cuz I didn't have nuthin' to hunt with. So, I had to lay out of the next night, which I did. And that night I found me a big fir tree and laid down and, directly as it got dark, here come that ole moon or new moon, can't remember which. But as that moon rose across the sky, it deposited my powder horn and my pouch back on that same tree limb.

"Well, the next day when I loaded up my rifle-gun to shoot her, I recken that old moon had picked up some nitro-glycereeen or something a—travelin' around the earth, cuz' when I went to fire her off, the gun barrel exploded! Half of it went over one side of a mountain and killed a bobcat and the other half went over the other side of the mountain and pinned five partridge to a log!"

And then, so the teller of the tale told me, Wiley Oakley yodeled!

Wiley Oakley was a painter of pictures, too. He was actually a very good primitive artist. Some of his landscapes are wonderful, charming paintings. He ran a little crafts store and raised a big family. Lucinda, his eldest daughter, would say he never worked too hard! Oh, she loved him and, when she spoke of Dad, she always smiled.

A friend to President and Mrs. Roosevelt and Henry Ford, he did much in playing his part to help make the Great Smoky Mountain National Park become a reality. In his own way, Wiley's contribution to the founding of the Great Smoky Mountains National Park is just as significant as anybody's, including Carlos Campbell and the great Jim Thompson. Without Wiley Oakley, as the Park's unofficial "public relations specialist," the National Park may not have happened.

"Rain, rain, Smoky Mountains is thy name," is something else Wiley used to say. It sure helps me

Storyteller and mountain guide, sad-eyed Wiley Oakley, the roamin' man of the mountains.

Wiley with Henry Ford (*second from right*), and other big shots.

Young ranger Glenn Cardwell.

An older, wiser, Glenn Cardwell.

when I go to the Smoky Mountains to remember that it's a temperate rain forest. Like Wiley says, it rains often, nearly every day. So, be ready.

One more famous Wiley Oakley quote is about him being lost in the mountains. Whenever he was asked if he got lost in the Great Smoky Mountains, Wiley's answer was always the same: "I twern't never lost, but I been mighty bothered!"

Glenn Cardwell

Glenn Cardwell, "the mayor of Pittman Center," as he came to be known, was the first Park employee we met in 1984. We were visiting the Park's Visitor Center in the Sugarlands, outside of Gatlinburg. Glenn was working the front desk as we walked in that day.

Our friendship has lasted more than twenty-five years. I know no better source of information about the people of the Smoky Mountains. Glenn was born in the Greenbrier section of the Park, before there was a National Park. At this writing, he still lives in Pittman Center with his lovely wife, Faye, just about five miles downstream from where he was raised. He's lived there for all the time I've known him.

Glenn has a scholar's mind, a scientist's technique, and the memory of an elephant. We've gone to him repeatedly for information about everything from early knowledge of the people of Greenbrier to genealogy, botany, animals, and Park trails. You name it, Glenn knows it.

My favorite memory with Glenn is hiking in Greenbrier, his favorite place on earth. We went up Injun Trail, or is it Engine Trail? There's an old boiler up there to see. On this trip, Glenn sang an old church song, "Working the Road to Glory."

It was Glenn's father-in-law, Oliver Huskey, who told us our most unforgettable panther tale. We'd just been to see Ray Hicks, who talked about his experiences with mountain lions or panthers. It's the eastern cougar, or puma, we're referring to. The last official panther sighting in the Park was in 1917 or so. But there have been numerous reports of mountain lions since, many recently.

We were interviewing Mr. Huskey for another project, and had talked with him for more than two hours when the subject came up. Doug had begun to pack up the lights and equipment. It was then I happened to ask Oliver if he'd ever heard of the ole mountain painters or if he knew any tales about them? "Aah," he said, "just one."

Doug looked at me, and even though it was late in the day, about 5:30, and we had an hour-and-a-half drive back to the station, he smiled, put the lights back up, and turned on the camera. This is the tale that Oliver Huskey told us. He said he first heard his grandfather tell it for the truth.

"The Panther & the Bear"

"One time, I was going huntin' up in the high mountains and I was away past our place, away up in the Smoky Mountains. I had my hog rifle, my pea rifle. Some folks call 'em my rifle-gun.

"I was away up in the high mountains. I was a coming thru the brush, when directly I come across a bubblin' brook. And there, by this big log, across the creek, I spied this big painter asleep on that log by that crick.

"Well, my grandfather said he hunkered down there behind this log to get a bead on that big painter. Just as he did, from behind him, he heared a rustle from the ivy there—the laurel, we call it.

"My grandfather said from out that ivy comes this BIG bear! I mean, a big one. My grandfather slunk down there behind that log to watch. That big bear spied the painter! He said that painter was asleep on that log and couldn't hear the big bear cuz of that creek. The big bear come acrost that bubblin' creek, and he drawed back that big paw and he took it and whacked that painter!

"He said that painter comes off that log, and he was in that crick. And he come outa that crick and then he was on that bear. And they went at it. THEY WENT AT IT! The big bear got a' holt of that big painter (here he was showing us, too,) and he squeezed him, and he squeezed him with them two big arms, and directly that big painter went limp, and that big bear just dropped him. And there lay that big painter. Dead. DEAD!"

Here, Mr. Huskey paused a long time, it seemed like. He had his arm out pointing down where that dead painter lay. Finally, after about four or five seconds, he continued. "That big bear was ripped from stem to stern from the back hind legs of that painter. And that bear sort of dragged its entrails down that trail a bit and into that ivy there, the laurel, we called it.

"My grandfather waited there a while and followed that bear into that laurel. And there lay that big bear, dead. DEAD! My grandfather skinned out a quarter hind end of that bear and took the hide back with him. He said he never knowed what became of the painter hide."

Then Mr. Huskey got up and went into the kitchen. Doug just turned and looked at me. We packed up the gear and got home about 8:30 that night.

"I twern't never lost, but I been mighty bothered!"
—Wiley Oakley

John Hendrix Prophecy

John Hendrix lived from 1865 until 1915 and was called "The Prophet." Around 1903 or so, he foretold the coming of Oak Ridge. That's about thirty-five years before anyone had any inkling of what uranium could do, or that it even existed. The land was just quiet East Tennessee countryside, made up of small farms. The area that became Oak Ridge was comprised of the small villages of Elsa, Wheat, Scarboro, and Robertsville.

Bear Creek Valley is what they called the land that became Y-12. In 1944, the farms south along the Clinch River became the site of the largest and longest building in the world. It even had bicycles inside for people to use.

People in Oak Ridge today can't explain it, but somehow the Prophet John Hendrix knew all of this was coming. Sometime around 1903, he's quoted as saying this, and saying it repeatedly:

"I tell you, Bear Creek Valley someday will be filled with great buildings and factories. They will help in winning one of the greatest wars that ever will be. There will be a city on Black Oak Ridge, and the center of authority will be on a spot middle-way between Sevier Tadlock's farm and Joe Pyatt's place.

"A railroad spur will branch off the main L&N line, run down toward Robertsville and then branch off, and turn towards Scarboro. Big engines will dig ditches and thousands of people will be running to and fro. They will be building things, and there will be great noise and confusion and the earth will shake. I've seen it! It's coming!"

Ray Hicks's Tales: "I Know I Talk Odd"

He had the purest old English accent in America, and was interviewed many times by Charles Kuralt and Charles Osgood of CBS. We were fortunate to meet him and his wife, Rosie, in 1987, atop their mountain abode near Boone, North Carolina. Ray's cabin overlooked the valley below and had a huge porch stacked with firewood for the winter. It was a beautiful fall day, and we sat under the overhang on his porch where we did the interview.

The impeccably clean cabin was in a spectacular setting near the Vera Cruz community, by the old Mast Store. That's where he learned to talk. Ray always said he goes back not to his father, but to his grandfather, Benjamin Hicks. "He cuud tell a tale hisself!"

Sean Kirk arranged for us to meet Ray through an East Tennessee State University Appalachian Folklore Department contact that helped us with "Our Native Tongue" story. As Doug recorded, Ray told some of the old Jack Tales, about that rascal Jack who could always outfox all the city fellers, the slickers. Jack had a natural gift for getting in and out of trouble, and escaped his troubles and predicaments by fantastic use of his own wit and trickery. They'd trick Jack in these tales, and he'd trick them back, only better.

The Jack Tales are famous mountain versions of the Uncle Remus Tales that feature Br'er Fox and Br'er Rabbit. The book *Jack Tales* might have been authored by someone else, but the stories are all Ray's.

We tried to document Ray's Jack Tales, but the stories go on for about twenty-five or thirty minutes each! An entire *Heartland Series* episode only

Ray Hicks's home in North Carolina.

lasts three minutes and forty seconds. Ray's Jack Tales just weren't much suited for our kind of TV.

Nevertheless, it was a day to remember. Ray talked about all kinds of other things. Some were terribly poetic, like his stories of plowing the new ground. For instance, he said, "Then the rains came—it'd come and warsh all the new ground off down into the valley!" I thought this story was so wonderful I developed it into its own story, which we aired and called, "A Peck to the Hill."

To describe the way Ray speaks, you have to see him. Imagine a big, tall mountain man with an old felt hat flopped atop his lanky frame. He looked like Ichabod Crane in the southern mountains, only taller.

When he talks, he leans over with every ounce of energy he has, and he nearly bursts with joy communicating every word, sound, and syllable to you. It's fun just to see him do it. He stresses every word.

He bubbles with enjoyment at performing a story. It feels like the story is for you alone. It doesn't matter how many are listening. You just know he's talking only to you. Like when he says, "Ray! RAY!! My daddy said, Raay, you go plant these seeds whar the grou-ond won't grow no

Abrams Creek and footbridge, W. O. Garner photograph, circa 1903.

weeeeds! Gyaaaw!! Whar the grou-ond won't grow no weeds: It won't grow no foood!

"They thought the ground was fertile! Just call it DIRT! They didn't know it had no richness of soil that God made the good earth, so. They didn't think they needed any fertilize. Ground was fertile—dirt! Now, I went back and used ashes. They didn't know the ground had no fungess, and richness to it. That's why they nearly starved so. My daddy did!"

Ray used the Middle English pronunciation of "hope" for help, and "hit" for it. He said, "I'm a-goin' and a-comin', a-singin' and a-sangin'." That is, singing a song and hunting the herb, ginsang. We found after much research that some of Ray's language usage can be traced to the great writer Geoffrey Chaucer's time in twelfth-century England. This led us to a series of southern mountain speech stories with linguists like Dr. Michael Montgomery and Dr. Gratis Williams of Berea,

Mountain cabin with family and visitors, W.O. Garner photograph, circa 1903.

Kentucky, whose monumental work *Southern Mountain Speech* was the first book on the subject we were able to find. Michael's book *Dictionary of Southern Mountain Speech* was written much later.

Ray could tell you a story about the weather. It was the dramatics of his delivery and the sound of his words and voice that were so special. We were asking him once if he ever heard of anybody seeing a panther, an eastern cougar, or mountain lion. We always wanted to prove the existence of the panther, and get a shot of it in the wild.

Immediately after the question, Ray scrunched up his face, and as dramatic as the best actor reciting *King Lear*, with his face all serious and frowned up, he said, "One layed me!!" I couldn't understand him. "What?" "One layed me!" I still didn't understand, but he continued to explain. "If'n it hadn't–a-been fer ma-grandfather a-teachin' me ta carry rocks in ma pocket, he'd a eat me up!"

That translates to, "If it had not been for my Grandfather teaching me to carry rocks in my pocket, he would have eaten me up."

Ray's speech is all about rhythm, rhyme, music, and the clippity, clippity clop of the percussives,

Stories, Tales, and Storytellers [101]

keeping the beat and playing the music of the line. Each word, each sound has a meaning. It may not even be intelligible or connected to a word, or even be a word. Oftentimes, Ray uses words that don't have a meaning. Like, in a particular Jack Tale, Jack says, "Soop buck, saaw buck, let's get to town!"

I don't know if that even HAS a meaning. I don't know what that means other than, "Hyaa! Mule!! Come on! Let's go!" But in the context of his stories, his tales, "Soop buck, saaw buck, let's get to town" works great. The listener knows exactly what he means, even though he's not using words to convey the meaning.

Instead, he often uses nonsense words, or sounds, and the dramatic presentation of them. It's a relatively common Appalachian story trait. Across the valley, up near Jamestown, another storyteller by the name of Johnny Ray Hicks of the singing Hicks family does this, too.

It's thrilling to hear. It's exciting because rarely has a listener heard anything like it before. It's a new language and you understand it. That's makes it fun, too.

Many of Ray's tales, some might say, are off-color. But linguists say that, in the use of mountain humor, we can get away with a bit more racy or suggestive material than in other forms of communication. What might be offensive without humor is more easily accessible to a broader audience with it. We sat on his porch and recorded Ray telling tales for two hours or more. He never missed a breath. Most of his stories we couldn't air on TV. Ha! But take my word for it, they are funny.

The joy is in seeing Ray tell the story. That's his unique way, his gift to us. Someday, you may get to hear more of Ray's tales. The original *Heartland* interview tapes are being collected and transferred to digital sound format at the East Tennessee History Center in Knoxville. The work is being done by Bradley Reeves and our friends at Tennessee Archive of Motion Image and Sound, TAMIS. There, they will be stored for posterity. Ray's stories alone make the salvage operation worthwhile.

Lessons aboard the Valley Adventure

From 1982 until near the end of 1983, I worked aboard the Valley Adventure for TVA. It was during this experience that I began to understand something of the people and the land of the Tennessee Valley. The Valley Adventure traveled to twenty-three ports along the Tennessee, Cumberland, and Mississippi Rivers from Knoxville to Memphis.

Opossums and Sweet Potatoes

It was aboard the Valley Adventure I first heard about a southern culinary delicacy, opossums and sweet potatoes. This is a story about how life and art are intertwined. I learned that opossums and sweet potatoes were staples in the diet of many southern mountain folks, but it's not just a southern country meal.

When speaking to large groups, often I'd ask people to raise their hands if they'd ever eaten opossum. Only about fifteen to twenty percent usually had. In East Tennessee, however, if you ask people how many had eaten "chitlin's," perhaps thirty percent would say "Yes," predominately in the older white congregations.

[Note: I mention this only because chitlin's is a mountain protein food not just a black soul food. In the mountains it was never about black

The Valley Adventure and the Maggie B head downriver after the World's Fair.

and white. It was about having something to eat. Opossums and sweet potatoes were eaten in the southern Appalachian Mountains, as well as the southern valley.]

"The Lord put the opossum on the earth, so we'd always have something to eat," is a wonderful line I first heard in Northern Alabama, but I've heard it in and around the Smoky Mountains as well.

We wanted to do a story about this southern mountain delicacy, but there were two problems. First, where do you find an opossum that's fit to eat? The second one is, once you find it you've got to eat it!

"The Lord put the opossum on the earth so we'd always have something to eat."

Now, eating the thing was my problem. I knew that from the start. Also, I don't like sweet potatoes. My grandmother cooked wonderful sweet potatoes, but I never ate them. I regret it now, because then at least I could enjoy half the meal.

So, with a "never say die" attitude we went ahead and tried to put this meal story together. It would be a cooking and eating show—our favorite kind. It seemed that no matter what we were eating, by the time we got around to shooting that part of the show, we were always so hungry, we'd eat anything. Opossum, we figured, wouldn't be any different.

Joan Wolf offered to help us. She grew up near Washburn on the other side of Clinch Mountain in Grainger County, and was raised in an area called Poor Valley near Puncheon Camp.

When Joan was young, her father loved to hunt opossum and other wild game. It was meat and something to eat. My Happy Valley neighbors, Abe and his Uncle Grady Whitehead, told me, "If you didn't grow it, trap it, catch it, kill it, skin it, or can it, you didn't eat." That was probably just as true for Joan Wolf's clan.

Joan grew up with eight sisters, all of whom "made school teachers," as she said. Her daddy hunted two or three nights a week to feed all his girls. That's how Joan learned to cook and eat opossum, and occasionally, still does.

She sure could cook a good opossum! But, of course, we didn't know the difference between a good one and a bad one. Like Effie Baker says, "We were raised to it." Joan says it a little different: "You can't get away from your raisin'." With that, she agreed to cook us a good wholesome *Heartland* meal of opossum and sweet potatoes—if we could catch one.

That's where ole Clay Graves came in. He lived up in Corryton, was a good friend of Joan's, and happened to raise rabbits. Clay agreed he could catch a big, fat opossum to eat, no problem.

It's a good thing, too, because we couldn't just go down to Bi-Lo or Food City and pick one up. You had to catch one. This was around August. One day when I came home to Bearden where I lived then, I found this little opossum inside my garage, barely ten inches long, plus his tail. When I got out of the car, I saw that rat looking thing. It was playing in the paint cans.

I grabbed a broom and ran it outside. A couple of weeks later, the same thing happened. There was an opossum in my garage. My father-in-law said, "Just grab him by the tail and throw him out of there. They don't have any muscles in their back. Just grab him and throw him out of your garage." So the next time I found him in there, I got a glove and did it. I felt good about it, too, like a real mountain man!

Well, as time passed, my wife began to be attracted to that opossum. I'd come home and she'd be talking to that critter hiding in the paint cans in the garage, "You better get out of here. Bill's going to get you! Go on!" She'd shoo that opossum out with the broom.

Clay Graves wasn't having any luck catching one. Meanwhile, that opossum in our garage was getting bigger and bigger! He was looking awfully good, too. By November or so, we needed to do the story. So, I told Clay Graves to give me his opossum trap. I know where we can get one. Ha! There's one hanging out in my garage!

So, I got the trap and that night put some cat food and peanut butter in it for bait, and set it out the back door of the garage. It was getting cold by then, and I thought the bait would surely entice that critter. The next day I got up early, went outside and checked the trap. I'd caught the neighbor's cat!

It was a big white Persian. Mad as the devil, too. You know what I'm talking about if you've ever tried to get a mad tom cat out of an opossum trap. It'll scratch you all to pieces.

I set the trap again and got up early the next morning before my wife. I'd caught that opossum! He was a big one. My wife asked me very suspiciously, "Where are you going with that opossum?" I said, "I'm going to take it to the country!" Well, I took it up to Corryton and gave it to Clay Graves. On the way out there, we stopped and got some Gerber baby food, a couple of jars of honey, and a pint of molasses.

Clay said we'd feed that to him to clean him out. Two weeks later, we shot the story "Opossum and Sweet Potatoes." Clay killed it and skinned it. We did the interviews. Joan cooked our opossum and sweet potatoes. It wasn't bad either. People ask me what opossum tastes like. I usually say, "It's like when you go to that little diner in Wartburg, the one that used to be open near the main road. If you go in there and have the lunch special—roast beef for $3.95—that's about what opossum tastes like. It's just a little greasier, but it's pretty good."

Three weeks later, after we'd finished and edited the show, my wife and I were getting dressed for work one morning, and one of the new *Heartland* episodes for the week came on. The title came up and it read: "Opossum and Sweet Potatoes." Well, that got my wife's attention.

She started looking at the TV and then kept looking back at me. She watched a little more of the story, turned, and looked at me. By this time, I was whistling, pretending not to know anything about anything!

Then she said, "Hey! Where'd you get that opossum?" I started stammering, like a kid about to wet his pants, and said something that sounded like: "I ya, I am, I ya, I ya." She said, "You told me you were going to take that opossum to the COUNTRY?" I said, "I took it to the country! I took it to Corryton." Then she asked, with a look I'd never seen before, "Did you kill that opossum?"

As she asked this, a more mature look of surprise and disappointment began to show through. What, a moment ago, was anger and disbelief was replaced with shock and awe! "You killed our OPOSSUM?" Then, she just looked pitifully at me and said, "Did you EAT our opossum?"

I remember stammering something about having taken the opossum to the country and that Clay Graves killed it, that I didn't kill it. I ate it, but I didn't kill it. I had to do it. It was my job, I tell you! That's the truth. But, I don't think she ever really believed me.

I'm telling this story for the truth. Well, most of it. Hee, hee, hee!

Making moonshine, around 1935.

CHAPTER II

Moonshine Stories and Halloween Tales

Making Liquor

Telling some of these tales is easier and much more fun than telling others. Some of them should be told, some I like to tell; and some, perhaps, shouldn't be told.

The Moonshiner's story is one that I like to tell. People enjoy it, so it's told often. The sad thing is that during the twenty-five-year run of the *Series,* we were called every month or so by TV producers in New York, L. A., Atlanta or some other place, hoping we could take their crews out and introduce them to a real moonshiner.

It's as if some media folks think that's all we have to offer, or the only thing the Appalachian people can do is make whiskey.

We knew from the beginning we were going to do a story on moonshine, but it wasn't until the third season that we did it. It wasn't very hard to find someone to teach us about liquor making. The problem was to find the right moonshiner.

Many of our favorite *Heartlanders* made "licker," or knew folks who did. Maynard Ledbetter talked about it. "Pot" Dorsey and other good folks in Cocke County told tales about it. That's how Mr. Dorsey got his nickname. He helped work an old still on his way to school in the morning, and often arrived late for school and covered in soot. So they started calling him "Pot."

He told us he did this as a little bitty feller. Then, by the ripe old age of ten, he drove a truck. They had to put a block of wood under his shoe so he could reach the pedals. He hauled sugar and fixin's for a few stills, and helped at different whiskey-making operations.

The story of moonshine is the struggle by some people in the Appalachians and other places to make a living. Making and selling liquor is not an easy way to provide for one's family. Every moonshiner we talked to said the same thing: "If we didn't have to make it, we wouldn't." It was too difficult a life and too dangerous a profession, although most of those we met took great pride in the quality of their particular creation.

The Moonshiner's Tale

Eulyss Roberts is the moonshiner we finally chose to talk to. He lived near Oliver Springs at the foot of Windrock Mountain.

We heard about him from a friend of a friend of the Assistant Deputy Sheriff of Anderson County. Just far enough back that our sources got a little hazy. Dealing with moonshiners and moonshine, you don't want to know too much about what's going on. You have to trust the people you're dealing with because they trust you. You can't ask too many questions until you know exactly where you are and who you're dealing with.

We trusted our sources and found Eulyss, pronounced "you-less." He lived down an old gravel road in a small house with a sofa on the front porch. The porch ran the length of the house, which had an overhang. When we drove up the road Eulyss was sitting on the old sofa on his porch in his pajamas.

He proceeded to tell us the name of every lawyer, judge, and sheriff in Anderson, Roane, and Morgan Counties that he'd sold liquor to. We always threatened to use that information if we ever needed to!

"Whiskey's made to sell. It ain't made to drink," he said. "Whiskey'll ruin the best man in the world. I know. I've drunk enough of it to climb a locust tree backerds."

Eulyss said he'd get up every morning and drink a pint of whiskey. Then, he'd eat a big breakfast and go to the coal mines. About 10:30 he'd get to shaking so bad he'd drink another pint. He said it took him thirty-five years to find out what it was doing to him, and when he did, he quit it.

He said he made a batch one time and, as he was running it through the still, something went wrong. "Something got clogged up in the worm, and the thump keg got to rattlin' real bad," he said, "so I jumped up on the thump keg and directly, Poof!" He made a sound to simulate the air blowing through a pipe or something.

He said, "The next day when I went to dump out the old mash and clean out everything, as I turned the keg over, I looked up and seen this mouse's head roll out of the mash leavins. Its eyeball was hanging out from the side of its head. It was the sickest thing I'd ever seen."

"What did you do with the whiskey?" I asked.

"Sold it," he said. Then he added quickly, "It ain't made to drink. It's made to sell."

Throughout the run of the *Series*, whenever we got word of the passing of one of our *Heartland* subjects, we always tried to pay our respects by putting a little font at the conclusion of the show. "In Memoriam," was a way to let the audience know the person was no longer alive and with us.

After rerunning "The Moonshiner" episode a few times we received a call from a friend or a family member informing us of Eulyss's passing. So, we tagged "In Memoriam" on the story for the next time it would run.

Well, about a year later we reran it, and promptly got a call saying "Eulyss isn't dead. He's alive!" That only happened one other time that I remember. As if that wasn't enough, more years passed and when we ran it again, we received another call saying that Eulyss had in fact passed on.

We put "In Memoriam" on the show again and aired it. And again we got another call saying that Eulyss is alive! So we don't know whether he's alive or not. Frankly, we think somebody out there is still drinking his mouse-head moonshine!

When we finished editing this 1985 episode, Steve wanted to get a second opinion. We weren't sure if the episode was too harsh, raw, to run on TV in Knoxville. How would our audience interpret it? Was it too edgy? Joe Cable, who also worked in the Promotions Department and helped edit many stories, thought it was bold, but not of-

"Whiskey's made to sell. It ain't made to drink."
—Eulyss Roberts

Old still by Maryville jail with Jake and Jim Garland (second and third from left), whose Daddy, Charlie, carried a 217-pound stove on his back from Maryville to the Beard Cane, near Cades Cove, a journey of at least seventeen miles, without even putting it down to rest.

fensive. So, we aired it, including the line about the mouse's eye dangling in the mash.

But that's not the end of the story. We still had to find something to show while Eulyss was telling the tale. We needed to find a working still and shoot it operating. Once again, Hal Watson came to our rescue.

Sevier County Sheriff, Carmen Townsend, was Hal's boss, a small man with a large reputation. He was a very funny man, and he and Hal were great friends. Hal said Carmen Townsend offered to set up his old still if we wanted to use it. Sean Kirk produced the show and they set it up somewhere near Sugarloaf Mountain, off Chapman Highway.

I couldn't be there, but watched the video after the shoot. It was terrific! Dramatically, it showed an exact operating still, churning out the liquor, with Hal in his overalls making it. There were even two or three other actors positioned around the still, helping to carry firewood or standing guard as a lookout.

When Sean asked Hal who those extra guys were, he smiled and said, "Sheriff Townsend said for us to take them with us. They were locked-up prisoners with nothing to do." Actually, they were pretty good actors, but then they weren't really acting. Hal said, "They knew an awful lot about it."

What a Pretty World

Nearly ten years later, we received a call from a Morgan County moonshiner, who explained he was using a hand-made, all copper still and the recipe of Morgan County's most famous liquor

CCC camp at the Sugarlands.

Black Will Walker and Old Death, his long rifle.

maker. He asked if we'd like to see how it's done and run a batch.

First, we checked with the ATF folks, the Bureau of Alcohol, Tobacco, and Firearms. They said it was still illegal, even to manufacture alcohol for one's own use. But they suggested if we were careful, and didn't show the "shiner's" face, it would be okay with them if we went ahead and did the show.

We shot the story and showed the moonshiner working, but only from the neck down. About three weeks after the show was edited and aired, Linda received a phone call from our "moonshiner." It was Thursday, the day he made liquor. He was extremely intoxicated and wanted Linda to have a drink with him. Of course, she declined. From then on, every Thursday, we'd take the calls and respectfully decline his invitation for someone to join him. He just didn't want to drink alone, I guess.

I remember something special he did and said, though. As he ran off a batch, he'd hold up the quart jar and shake it. Then, he'd just stare at the bubbles for a long time. Finally, with a serene sense of wonder, he'd say, "What a pretty world! What a pretty world!"

It's true that a good liquor maker can tell the proof within five percent; simply by shaking a jar and watching the bubbles rise. The run he made with us was 190 proof. He would cut it later, to weaken or smooth it down to 90 proof, or so. It wasn't the alcohol content that our moonshiner was looking for. When he shook a jar and looked at the bubbles, he was looking for that imaginary place where it took you when you drank it. "What a pretty world!"

Halloween Tales

Halloween is for children. That's why we loved it so much. It's one of our favorite holidays of the year and it isn't even an official holiday. Schools are open, and you don't do anything special except try to scare people and try to be scared yourself.

Our first Halloween tale was called "Haints." It was a good story, a grandfather's tale about the Smoky Mountains. Laura Armour, our producer, was great as the dead lady who comes back with a milk pail to get cream for her baby. Hal Watson played the farmer who follows her to the gravesite, and I played Kiley Eller with my hat pulled down so you couldn't tell it was me.

The story is about saving the woman's young child who was buried with her. Like any good scary story, it has a great opening line, "For two days the mountain sky had been weeping, like a newborn baby for its mother." Steve wrote this story. Like, "It was a dark and stormy night," or "Once upon a midnight dreary," the mood is set and the audience knows what the story is about.

There are a few archetypical tales we've all heard growing up in this region. Around Hamblin County, to scare children into doing what they're supposed to do, folks say, "You better do it or Rendy Bailey will get you!"

Rendy was an old wandering crone, actually a real person who wandered homeless, like a bag lady, and often slept in a fence row. Occasionally she'd appear, shake an old tin cup, and say, "Coppers! Do you have any coppers to spare?" She was looking for spare change.

Ghost, Doug, me, Sam Moore, and Victor Porter (behind Sam) on location, shooting a Halloween tale.

Jasper Mellinger's Tale

Jasper Mellinger's story is another oft-told tale, around the Smokies where it happened a little after the turn of the century. It's one of the saddest tales told around these mountains.

Oh, Jasper was real, all right. He lived up Roar-

Moonshine Stories and Halloween Tales [111]

ing Fork Creek outside of Gatlinburg, not too far above Herb Clabo's place. Jasper's life was being rained on, so to speak. He was going through a bad time and desperately needed work as one of his daughters had died of consumption, or tuberculosis.

Jasper heard they were hiring blacksmiths and timber cutters in North Carolina, so he left for Gatlinburg, then on to Elkmont, then up over the mountain to North Carolina to see about it.

At Ogle's Store in Gatlinburg, Charlie loaned him his shotgun, and he spent the night in Elkmont at Lem Ownby's place. The next morning he said goodbye to Lem and started over the mountains. There was a heavy mist and a thick fog on the trail.

No one ever saw Jasper Mellinger alive again. He never made it back home. In fact, he never made it across the mountains. About three years later, 1906 or so, Wiley Oakley was nosing around the mountains and came upon the rotted remains of a skeleton of a man caught in a bear trap! They also identified Charlie Ogle's old shotgun, and found what looked to be Jasper's spectacles, and a Bible he never went anywhere without. That's how they identified the body.

What happened next was told to us for the truth. I've removed the names because I'm not sure who committed the crime. After the body was found by Wiley, one of the people involved in the incident came down deathly sick. We'll call him Sully Boy. On his death bed, the Sully Boy confessed to having a hand in Jasper's death.

Court testimony confirms Sully Boy and his father admitted setting their bear traps too close to the trail. However, in the fog and mist, Jasper lost his way and stumbled into the trap; but that didn't kill him.

Sully Boy said he found Jasper two or three days later, still alive, but with a broken leg and half dead. According to the story, the boy asked his paw what he ought to do. The old man said, "Just take a pine knot to him and leave him." So that's what the Sully Boy did.

Then, the story takes a strange turn, because after confessing on his deathbed to what they did to Jasper, the Sully Boy did not die! Instead, he was arrested. They lawed 'em, which was the mountain term for bringing him and his father to trial in a court in Sevierville.

They dumped the bones of Jasper Mellinger right on the floor in front of the judge. The older Sully man and his son, who had recovered, were both acquitted of Jasper's murder. There wasn't enough evidence.

Nearly twenty-two years ago, I first heard that Wiley Oakley had once found the skeleton of a man caught in a bear trap. It wasn't until ten or fifteen years later I learned the skeletal remains were those of Jasper Mellinger. It's interesting how these stories are all connected.

If you look on the Park Service maps of the Great Smoky Mountains over toward the Elkmont area, you will see a mountain ridge named, "Mellinger Death Ridge." This is where the remains of poor Jasper were found.

The Mellinger family had a difficult time surviving. Mrs. Mellinger, I read, lived for a time in some government-assisted housing in Sevierville toward the end of her life. We talked to a descendant of Jasper Mellinger. He showed us Jasper's old spectacles and the remains of Charlie Ogle's half-rotted shotgun.

But we didn't do this story. The decision was made that there were just too many Sully family members alive, and it was thought the story might

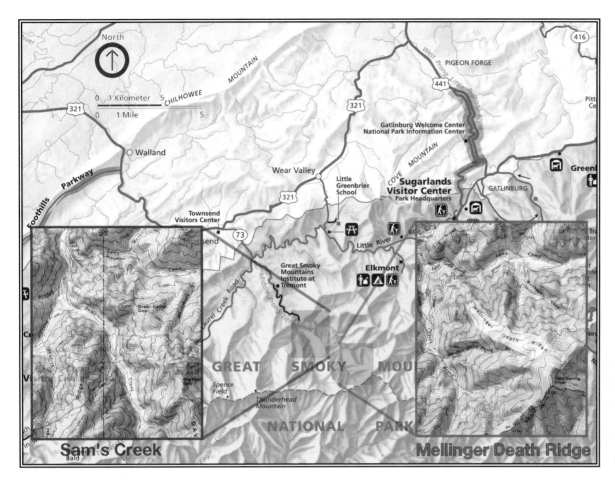

Map showing the location of Mellinger Death Ridge. It's located not far from Elkmont and is the place where Wiley Oakley found the remains of Jasper Mellinger three years after Jasper disappeared.

be offensive to many good folks. It was decided, rather, to let the story lie with old Jasper.

I'm telling it now because it's always bothered me. It's a tragic tale where an evil act occurred and possibly went unpunished. The Mellinger family never found restitution and suffered for generations because of it. Perhaps that's the reason the old map makers named that ridge after Jasper.

The Witches Curse—Thelma Mathis's Story and Superstitions

I'm telling you the truth. Right here, there are some of the most superstitious folks you've ever seen in your life. One lady said, "If you borrow salt, you give me sugar. It's bad luck to bring back salt. If you bring a broom in the house, don't sweep under the bed! Oh no! If you come back into the house with a hoe, oh Lord, take it back out, it's bad luck."

Moonshine Stories and Halloween Tales [113]

Doug makes a point during the shooting of "13," a Halloween tale. That's another ghost on the left.

I absolutely loved one teller of superstitious tales, Thelma Mathis. She lived by herself in a big old house in Oakdale, Tennessee. I think she had nine brothers and sisters. They all grew up in "Catoosie," as she called it, the Catoosa Wildlife Management Area up in Cumberland and Morgan Counties.

The day we met Thelma, she was trying to catch a huge six-foot black snake that had scurried under her dining room bureau. It was hiding among dozens of canned goods. We hoped to talk to Thelma alone about 'haints,' and later, talk again with her and her sister, Miss Pete.

We found her on her knees trying to catch the snake. She hollered for us to come on in. We saw the snake and moved every canned object in the house trying to catch it. Larry, her musician son, came by and helped, but we didn't have any luck. We finally gave up and went on and did the interview with Thelma, a magical lady. "Oh well," she said. "It won't hurt nuthin!"

Thelma's sister, Miss Pete, was married to "Pistol" Pete Burge, the High Sheriff of Morgan County. Miss Pete would give prisoners the evil eye, and that's all it took to get them back inside the jail if they happened to step out for something. Miss Pete did the cooking and rarely ever locked the cell doors in the jail house.

Back in 1987, Thelma shared some of her knowledge of superstitions and witches with us. I remember one tale about Dit Rose, a witch. "Up in upper East Tennessee around Tazewell was where the Roses lived, Joe Rose and Bill Rose and Uncle Jim, who was our pastor. His wife was in a wheel chair. She couldn't read nor write. We called her Aunt Barth, and she was part Indian, and I mean she was a doozy!

"Aunt Barth told about a witch up there in East Tennessee and she was adamant about it, too. I don't mean half way. She was one of 'em. She'd put spells on cows and horses and people and everything."

According to Thelma, Aunt Barth told her how to be a witch. "Aunt Barth told this tale about a young girl up in that country that wanted to be a witch. She said to go down to the river before the sun rises and stand there till the sun comes up, draw a circle in the dirt, stand in it, and you curse God and tell the devil that you're gonna work for him."

And she said, "They'll be a handkerchief come

A smiling, young Cas Walker, with Panhandle Pete next to him, pose before performing on Channel 10's *Farm and Home Hour.* **The banjo player is Willie Brewster.**

into your hand with a drop of blood on it. And you eat that drop of blood and you'll be a witch. So, she done that. And then she went back to the old witch and she said, 'Okay, let's try you out.'

"So she put spells on dogs and cats and things like that, you know and said, 'You're a witch now.'"

I asked Thelma, "What kind of spells would she put on?" and Thelma said, "She'd go through a chanting rigmarole or something, you know? And she'd say, 'Now you're going to be able to do this and your gonnna be able to do that.' And she said, 'And I will that the neighbor's cow over there not give any milk ever again. And dogs would go mad, and stuff like that'."

I asked Thelma "What about you and your sisters? Were you all superstitious and scared of witches and things like that?"

"Nope," Thelma said straight out, matter of fact like. "We wasn't any of us scared of them."

We tried to talk Steve into letting us do a story called the 'Witches Curse,' based on the tale told to Thelma by Aunt Barth. But he said the idea of

Moonshine Stories and Halloween Tales [115]

reenacting a young girl "cursing God and telling the devil that she wanted to work for him," was just too much like a "slasher movie."

Religion and politics were to be avoided at all cost in the *Heartland* world of TV. Nothing good could come of it—except we might be "sceered" and scare others, which were always our objectives in telling a good Halloween tale.

Many of these tales, we found, are based in nature and nature's mysteries. For years, superstitions were passed along to help explain natural world occurrences that otherwise couldn't be understood. Such as, "Why does a dog go mad?" Scientifically, we know now that it's rabid, but if you didn't know that, it must be explained, at least to yourself, by some other means.

Superstitions and tales of other worldly beings—held firm by some in these mountains—are a result of rich oral traditions. Simply put, they make for good stories.

Last year I re-met Larry Mathis, Thelma's son, after nearly twenty years. It turned out that Larry and his longtime partner, Bud Brewster, played with Dolly Parton on the old *Cas Walker Farm and Home Hour*, back in the early days of Channel 10 live TV in the late 1950s and 60s. We recently featured Larry and Bud as the house musicians in "Appalachian Dreams," a benefit concert for the Princess Theater Foundation that I hosted at Roane State Community College.

I was fortunate to see Larry and reminisce about his mother and wonderful family after so many years. It truly is a small world.

CHAPTER 12

World War II Tales

These stories on World War II could easily have been left out of this book. All I know is these tales should be remembered and shared. They are valuable.

It's been a blessing to have these good people tell them, to meet these great human beings who lived and fought to save everything we hold dear. I'm sure when the *Series* began, there was no plan to find, interview, and produce a series of stories about the home front of a world at war.

There is no rhyme or reason as to how we chose or found them. They just fell into our sphere of contact. I'm sorry we didn't do stories on many others who might have been just as deserving or even might have made better stories. It was serendipity. I wish it was more profound than that.

That's why I'm writing this book. Sure, mine is a skewed view. But, that's the only view I've got! But, I'm telling these stories for the truth, and these Second World War stories belong here.

There was a lady from Knoxville whose young husband was in the Navy fighting overseas during the war. She and a friend decided to go to the movies. While there, she happened to catch the newsreel feature that depicted the actual sinking of a Navy ship. Horrifically, it was her husband's carrier ship at sea!

On the screen in front of her, his ship was being attacked and blown apart. She realized it was his ship and he was on it. She saw it sink on the newsreel, while in the movie house. It was the first time she'd heard or seen anything about it. She was shocked and horrified. Can you imagine that? That's what happens at home in war.

Or, try to imagine a college, maybe the University of Tennessee. It is fall semester, 1941, and classes are full. Students are drinking beer, eating goldfish, or whatever else they do on Friday nights. By the January semester, immediately after the bombing of Pearl Harbor, eighty percent of all the men in your class, boys really, are gone; swept off to war.

At Doyle High School, maybe also Carter, upon graduation, the entire high school football team loaded into pickup trucks and drove straight to the enlistment office: the entire team enlisted. The winds of war were blowing and East Tennessee, the Volunteer State, responded—as it always did.

Dorothy Kiggans, Lenoir City

Dorothy Kiggans had just graduated from high school. She worked after school and on weekends

A young Dorothy Kiggans.

at the local five-and-dime drug store. She'd been working there for years. She knew almost everyone that came in and what they came to get. It was a little store in a small town in East Tennessee. There were hundreds of towns just like it, and maybe a thousand southern girls just like her. Well, not quite like Dorothy.

When the war broke out, she found herself on the other side of the country working in the Seattle shipyards. It was the time of Rosie the Riveter and somehow this shy Loudon County girl found herself dressed in a pair of overalls, with a hard hat, working as an electrician's assistant. She helped build ships for the navy's war effort.

Usually, men did this work, but there weren't any. They were all overseas. It wasn't that anyone was consciously thinking about women's lib; it was simply that there were boats to build, a war to win, and we needed to get to it. That was Dorothy's attitude and the feelings of most Americans.

On weekends and on an occasional day off, Dorothy and her friends would slip across the Canadian border and buy shoes. They'd hide their old ones or ship them home. Then, they would scuff up their brand new shoes and wear them back across the border.

Dorothy so enjoyed telling this to us. Later, I happened to meet a close friend of hers, an eighty-year-old gentleman who lived near her. He laughingly retold this tale. There was great joy in the telling of it.

When her ship, the USS Mobjack, was just about completed and ready for its maiden voyage, all the women were asked to leave the ship. It was customary that no woman ever sailed in the United States Navy. But shy little Dorothy Kiggans had learned a thing or two since leaving the old farm, and she wasn't about to miss the maiden voyage of her ship.

So Dorothy became the first American woman to sail on an American Navy ship, but she wasn't thinking about that. No, she wanted to be treated the same as all the other ship workers. Dorothy and a friend and co-worker stowed away on the maiden voyage! Hiding in the electrician's storage room, they didn't show themselves until it was too late for the ship to turn back. The crew had to keep them aboard for the entire week-long training mission.

Dorothy was in her eighties when we met her. Each time she'd tell her story, she'd laugh when she thought about her moment of victory. It was her brave contribution to winning the war. She was rewarded, too. At war's end, she returned to Loudon County. With the money she'd saved working in the naval shipyard, she built a nice home where she lived for the rest of her good, long life.

Dorothy's picture and electrician's badge from Seattle shipyards.

Luther Woods, Sharps Chapel

Luther Woods was a seventeen-year-old, tow-headed, strapping country boy who lived in Sharps Chapel with his twelve brothers and sisters. His story is more typical of East Tennesseans at war.

Luther's friends called him Lon, and he was a good friend to me. I liked him a lot. His was my favorite of the World War II stories we were fortunate to feature. Two of Lon's brothers served also, and Lon recalled looking all over Europe for one of them. He didn't know where his brother was, so everywhere he went, he looked for him and, one day, found him eating in a mess tent! He would cry just thinking about it.

I liked Lon because I understood him a little. I had four brothers, too, and can't imagine fighting a world war and not knowing whether any of them were alive or would ever come home again.

Sharps Chapel is a peninsula surrounded by Norris Lake now. It is located north on Highway 33 in Union County, about twenty-five miles from Knoxville. Lon spent his first night away from his mother's home, along with thirty-five other seventeen- and eighteen-year-old boys, in the barracks at Ft. Oglethorpe, Georgia.

There, he received his uniform and was told to put it in his footlocker. "Hell," he said, "I didn't know what a footlocker was!" He'd never seen a footlocker or even heard anybody talking about one. He'd never left Sharps Chapel before. He said, "They lined us up in our underwear and headed us soldier boys down the corridor. A door would open on the right, and somebody'd give us a shot in one arm, then another door would open and we'd get a needle in the other arm. It was a long hall!"

First seven of the thirteen Woods' children. Lon is third from left on back row in overalls.

I asked Lon what he thought when they first checked his prostate. He grinned at me, and instantly shook a big finger and said, "Right then, I learned how to take orders!" He laughed and laughed about that. He was a big man, six feet two inches tall and weighing two hundred and fifty pounds when we met him. He was having trouble with his leg and didn't move around much.

What a great day we had. Lon showed us a beautiful pearl-handled revolver he took off a German general who wanted to trade it for some cigarettes. "Did you trade with him?" I asked.

Luther (Lon) Woods in his uniform.

Lon later in life when we met him.

"No, I just took the pistol. Kicked his butt and sent him down the road."

In training, Lon's company wasn't allowed to eat at the same time as the northern recruits. They had to keep them separated because they'd always fight, Yankees against the southern boys. "It was because they thought they knew everything! You know how they are, Bill? Those Yankees, they think they know everything and are better than we are! We'd fight all the time."

Lon was a tremendous marksman, sharpshooter, and recorded the best shooting scores the army recorded during training for World War II. His scores were even comparable to Sergeant York's. "You know, Bill," he said, "You take a half dozen Yankees from New York who never fired a rifle, and put 'em up against a bunch of southern boys from Kentucky who'd never fired a gun either. And the southern boys would outshoot them every time. It's just in their blood to shoot."

He was the first man in his company to capture a German soldier, and somehow a picture of him made it to the *Knoxville Journal*. He showed it to us, a picture of a skinny Lon leading a general out of the woods in the Ardenne Forest.

Lon finished the war a sergeant. After the war, they didn't talk about PTSD—post-traumatic stress disorder—or have treatment for it. Shell-shocked veterans managed the best they could. He said he went home and worked the farm with his father, plowing the ground, and healing that way. About a year later, his brother came home and took up helping around the farm. Lon moved to Knoxville and went to work for Kerns Bakery.

Recalling his final home coming at the end of his long service, he said he'd taken a bus up from Knoxville, and got off with his duffel bag on the Maynardville Highway. He walked the last eight miles into Sharps Chapel thinking of all those things he'd seen and done. When he came over the ridge and across his family's fields, he could see his mother's farm house again. He'd made it. He saw his brothers and sisters on the porch, and they came running to meet him.

In telling Lon's story, we wanted to shoot the homecoming scene, and were looking for costumes for our actors to portray Lon, a few soldiers, and a brother or two.

We went down to the World War II museum on Chapman Highway, and were excited to find dozens of army uniforms we could use. When we checked the sizes to fit our actors, however, we were shocked. We found none of the pants would fit our actors. The sizes of these real uniform pants were 28, 30, and 32. There was one pair of 34s.

Suddenly, it all became real—the emaciated physical condition of these returning war heroes, how skinny they were when the war was over. We had to recast the show because the seventeen- and eighteen-year-old young men we'd cast to play Lon and his brothers couldn't fit into the costumes. They were way too big. We had to use fifteen- and sixteen-year-old boys to play the parts. It was an eye opener, all right. Of everything we learned about this period, this was the most shocking.

Ken Russell of Maryville and Benton, Tennessee

Ken Russell was an interview I didn't want to do. Of course it was pride. My feelings were hurt that I didn't find him, or know a little more about him before we did the interview. We'd been on the phone talking to many war veterans and I would've liked to call and talk to Ken before the interview.

The next thing Doug and I knew, we were heading down the highway near Maryville, along Topside Road, to meet this guy. I'd been told he was a World War II vet, and a lot had been written about him.

Well, Kenneth Russell, it turns out, was a major source for Stephen Ambrose's well-researched, monumental work, *Citizen Soldiers*. Not to mention the fact that Red Buttons actually portrayed Ken Russell in the classic World War II film, *The Longest Day*.

Ken Russell is one of the two guys who parachuted onto the church steeple at Sainte-Mère-Église, France. His parachute got hung in the bell tower, and he dangled from the roof. That's Ken Russell, the same guy who grew up in Benton, Tennessee, near Tellico Plains.

He was just a red-faced kid, star blocking back on Conasauga's football team as a sophomore. He wanted action, so he had his parents sign for him, and he joined the army as a sixteen-year-old. He moved to the paratroopers because he wanted more action. Well, he got his wish.

At 5:30 a.m., as the rest of the company washed and shaved, he and another young soldier were wrestling around the latrine, playing grab ass. That's when he heard a familiar voice screaming his name. It was their general. Young Russell didn't know he was in there. The general yelled, "Quit horsing around and get over here and shave like the rest of the men!" Russell said, "Sorry, general, we can't. We don't shave, yet." "Well," the general blustered, "Get over here! And act like you're shaving!"

The night of his high school prom, June 6, 1944, while the rest of his high school classmates were dancing with their high school sweethearts, Kenneth Russell jumped out of an airplane over Normandy Beach, during the invasion of France! That's why he landed on the church steeple in Sainte-Mère-Église. It was D-Day, and he was fifteen miles away from his targeted drop zone and landed in a German-occupied village.

As they floated to the ground, Germans ran outside, shooting, and killing thousands of paratroopers. Russell told me the story matter-of-factly. "Jumping out of that airplane was like jumping into hell," he said. "The whole world was exploding! Fires burned and bombs were exploding everywhere. It drew all the oxygen, and sucked paratroopers, just young boys, pulling them into those infernos, those massive fires."

Ken Russell was lucky; he missed the fires, but he still descended, as if in slow motion, giving him time to watch German soldiers shoot his buddies as they helplessly floated to earth.

He had a great, confident, smile, and a reddish hue about him. Over the years, much grey had crept into his dark brown hair. There was a warm friendliness, a worldliness about him, like he was glad to talk to us, if it would help us. I can see how Red Buttons could be cast as him, although the real Ken Russell was tall and lean.

He pulled out a box of medals, looking for a picture of General George Patton that he was more proud of than his medals, and he had a bunch of those. Patton always bragged he would pee in the Rhine when they entered Germany. "Let me show you something," Ken said, as he reached under the medals and pulled out the picture.

It was old, but carefully he showed it to us. It appeared to have been taken by a soldier with an

Ten-year-old Ken Russell.

Kenneth Russell in uniform.

old army Kodak. It was a low angle shot of Patton above the crowd. He was standing on a Jeep or something with hundreds of soldiers around him. He could have been on a bridge, or on a vehicle; but, anyway, there he was big as life, smiling General George Patton peeing in the Rhine. Ken Russell laughed and said, "All the soldiers called him "Shorty" after that!"

Ken died in 2004, exactly sixty years to the minute from the time he parachuted into France. He was a great source for World War II information. You can find out about him by checking the indexes of Stephen Ambrose's books, as well as others. He knew Major Richard Winters and other characters from Easy Company; citizen soldiers, who appeared at many veteran's events. Most were written about in *Band of Brothers* and other documentaries of World War II.

I was fortunate to meet him. I'm thankful for the chance to learn about these heroes and their personal experiences in World War II. Perhaps, it might keep us from rushing into other wars. It's always interesting to note, the last ones that actually vote to go to war are usually the ex-soldiers and veterans, those that fought in past wars. They know what it means. That's why it's to be avoided at all costs.

Unlike Ken Russell, many other veterans didn't start talking about their experiences until very late in their lives. Some never did.

A Funeral for a Veteran

As for my family, throughout all our childhood and teenage years, I can't recall my father telling us about World War II and his experiences, except for one story.

He said it was at Christmastime, when a German Messerschmitt or some kind of aircraft strafed his platoon. The plane came in low, blasting with a machine gun, bullets flying. My father said he was in his underwear and jumped in a foxhole full of water. He always smiled when he told this story.

He was close to seventy-four years of age when he died. All eight of my brothers and sisters gathered around the gravesite. It was one of those nasty, cold, grey winter days in Pennsylvania where we buried him.

Being a veteran, he was given a military stone marker at the foot of his grave. One of my brothers or sisters gave me a sheet of paper, an official looking document that came in the mail at his death. It was his military record. It listed his theaters of war and the medals and awards he'd received. They included "The Ardennes," and "The Battle of the Bulge."

Damn, I remember thinking, "the Battle of the Bulge!" My father fought there. I never knew that. My whole life, he never told me; he never told any of us.

CHAPTER 13

Real People

Struggling to describe what exactly *The Heartland Series* was about over the years, I found that we did four different types of stories:

1. Adventure Stories—where we went somewhere and saw something. Maybe we built a Clinch River boat or explored the natural beauty of Reelfoot Lake.
2. Reenactments—where actors helped us tell historical dramas, an April Fools story, a Halloween tale, or maybe a reenactment of the life of a historical character, such as Sequoyah, Davy Crockett, or John Sevier.
3. Science—we'd find out about cicadas, kudzu, or why a bee stings, the red wolves' reintroduction, rainbow trout, wild boar, life in the canopy, life in Little River, the bog, and shows like that.
4. Real People—like, A.D. and Walter Bohanon, Oma Lewis, Johnny Ray Hicks, Jack Sharp. We'd feature stories about these wonderful, unique people. Maybe they worked as a park ranger, teacher, scholar, or farmer. They were people you know, the special people we call *Heartlanders*.

Kim Delozier

The first time I met Kim Delozier, I didn't like him very much. I guess I didn't understand him. We wanted to do a story on European wild boar, and called the Great Smoky Mountains National Park asking for the wildlife people.

It was my first call to the National Park. Let's say I was inexperienced, though if you say, ignorant, you'd be just as correct. Kim Delozier got on the line. I was thinking about a guy named Kim. That's kind of like Sue, isn't it? "That's odd," I was thinking. "Isn't that a girl's name?"

"We were wondering if you or somebody would help us do a story on wild boar," I said very politely.

There was a long pause. Finally, he said, "How many are we talking about? How many people are in your crew?"

"Three, maybe," I said. "One is small."

There was another long pause. "Sure. Meet me at Newfound Gap, at 9:00 p.m. Thursday night, and we'll go out on a trail. We've had some hog sightings nearby. We'll try to get you some pictures of hogs."

John Carson and dogs hunting wild boar in Jeffries Hell.

Kim Delozier.

Oh boy! Our first Park camera shoot with a real ranger, and at night, too! Hey, we thought, that's about six thousand feet high up top of the mountain on 441 and our first mountain hike. Wow! We were excited.

We met Kim and hiked a trail and kept hiking. We made it all the way to Ice Water Springs. For the first time, we found out how heavy and awkward carrying TV equipment could be; especially uphill for long stretches at a time. We'd carry something on one shoulder for a minute or two, and then try the other one. It didn't matter which shoulder we used.

We found out, too, that we were not dressed for this. Some of us wore loafers. We had one windbreaker for the three of us. Man, it gets cold up there at night! We had no idea the weather changes so dramatically in the Park.

John Davis went on that first trip with Sean, Doug and me. John was a bright, creative guy, smart as a whip, but he wasn't too physical. At 6 feet 2 inches and about a hundred and fifty pounds, he was long, and skinny. I think John would agree this hike wasn't something he was born to do, but he wasn't the only one. We were ill-prepared, ill-equipped, and just didn't have a clue. We didn't even bring a flashlight.

Doug had his trusty Boy Scout pack, with dust

still on it. It was full of heavy batteries and tapes. With no frame, it cut into his shoulders badly. Gear was lashed to us like we were pack horses.

When we walked we sounded like a second grade rhythm band, banging and clanging so every critter within two miles of us disappeared, even some dead ones. Finally, Kim says, "Hey, let me go on ahead, you guys are making too much noise. I'll just go on up." And he left us, three or four miles from Newfound Gap, alone and without a light. Yikes! Onward we pressed, slowly, as in our minds these wild mountains were full of bears, wild boar, rattlesnakes, and panthers!

After about fifteen minutes, we'd covered another half-a-mile of trail. Just as we were coming around a giant spruce tree, we heard the horrible sounds of a wild boar rooting. It was right next to us, too. On top of us, I mean close. In fact, it was right behind that tree.

Just as we were ready to scream, drop our gear, and make a run for it, Kim stepped out from behind the tree and started laughing. Ha. We were so relieved we weren't something's dinner; we didn't get mad, though we may have soiled our clothes. After our hike, we gladly returned to the world.

Sitting at the old Howard Johnson's coffee shop in Gatlinburg at 3:00 in the morning, the cup of coffee sure tasted good; but we didn't have a single picture, not even one usable shot. We went home dejected and were back at the station at 8:00 a.m. Kim called about 9:30, asking if we were still looking for pictures of wild boar. This time I thought for a long minute and responded very, very carefully. "Yeah. Why?"

"Because," he said, "there's a four-hundred-pound old male pig in a two-acre, fenced-in pen, right behind the Sugarlands ranger station. If you

come back up, you probably could get some good shots in there."

We were there by 11:00. It took a lot more work, but the story, "European Wild Boar," included the great video we got that day. It was the first time we'd ever seen a real, wild boar running in the National Park. And we shot it running and close-up. It was built like a tank, no predators.

Wait a minute! Something wasn't exactly right here. On the way home it finally dawned on us. "Hey, that wild boar was in that pen yesterday, too." That means it was there last night, while we climbed those eight miles in the dark, with all that gear. I've never asked Kim about that trip in the twenty-four years since. I'm not exactly sure why he took us on that wild goose chase. But I think I have an idea.

Documenting the red wolf reintroduction with Gary Henry.

Grabblin'

Gene Patterson, who worked at Channel 10 before he became News Anchor on Channel 6, might have done a story on "Grabblin'," maybe even with George Moses, but it didn't matter. We wanted to go with George anyway. I found his phone number, called him up, and asked if we could go with him to catch big catfish by hand. I can assure you, I didn't have any idea what we were actually getting into, but it didn't take long to learn. George couldn't have been friendlier or easier to talk to. "Sure," he said. "Just call me back when it gets hot."

So I called him back at the end of June, and he said to call him back after the 4th of July. So I called him again, and he said to call him back about the 12th of July, which I did. That's when he said, "We're going Thursday!"

Now, it's interesting that someone knows so much about the habits of a creature to know precisely when to do this, to go "grabblin" for catfish. At the hottest time of the year, catfish will back into small crevices and little caves and look for a date. It's spawning time in Tennessee! So sometimes you can reach your hands in there and pull two catfish out of the same hole. At least, that's what these guys were telling us.

We met on Watts Bar Lake, off the main channel of the Tennessee River. Quickly, we were on the water looking for rocky ledges and bluffs where they said fish would be. We had two boats, one with George, the oldest of the crew, and one with his sixteen-year-old grandson, the youngest. Along, also, were two or three of George's nephews. They didn't wear bathing suits. They dressed like they were going to the mall; jeans and tennis shoes.

A typical catfish.

Doug put the one-thousand-dollar microphone on this big fella, who weighed about two hundred and sixty pounds. We drove up to what looked like the right habitat, off the main channel, with rocky shelves for the fish to hide in. It looked like ideal catfish spooning habitat to me.

Immediately, the big guy with the microphone strapped to his shirt stood up and jumped in. Yikes! I thought Doug Mills was going to jump in after him. "No, no!" But it was too late. Oh well, we still had one more microphone, and the camera mic. So, we weren't out of sound—yet.

(Note: When we shoot near water, Doug always uses condoms to keep the mics dry, but it's always a bit dicey when he turns in his expense report. The bean counters/accountants at the station are the only folks who know what a wild, partying animal Doug Mills really is—I'm kidding, of course! I'm not sure if Doug invented this technique or not. During World War II, soldiers would use condoms to keep the barrels of their rifles dry. Winston Churchill was approached once to sign off for the purchase of thousands of crates of condoms. No one else would vouch for the expenditure. Churchill had no problem signing for it, but he insisted that each crate and box on all future shipments would be printed with: "For British Soldiers" and the size: "EXTRA LARGE!")

Quickly, George and his boys latched on to some big cats, with mouths so big you could stick your entire hand in them. That's how you do it. Reach into a catfish's mouth, turn one's hand, grab him by the gills, and pull him out of there. "Try that!"

Catfish don't have teeth per se, but have tiny cilia that force food down their throats, like snakes' fangs. The difference is catfish have hundreds of these little fangs. They are angled backwards, so when catfish bite down on your hand, if you don't pull your hand out, it doesn't hurt.

One guy said, "It feels like the water temperature in the hole or cave drops about ten degrees, and you just know you're gonna get bit." I tried it, but I didn't get too far. We were in deep water, close to the bank, but could stand up. Everyone was bunched up together, because there was plenty of fish right there.

They were feeling their way along the bank and showed me what to do. I reached my hand down through these rocks. My head was out of the water and I'd turn my head a little, and reach down until I could feel the spiney dorsal top fin on the back of the catfish. I continued feeling my way down it until I could feel the body of the **WHOLE** catfish connected to it. It was a **HUGE CATFISH**!

How big? I'll tell you how big! A catfish is shaped like a football, and the part I was feeling at the base of the fin should have been rounded, right? I should have been able to feel an inch or two to the right of the fish and feel where its shape begins to curve. There was no curve in this fish. His back was straight across, level, as far as I could feel. Do you know how frightening that is?

I like my right hand. I've had it for fifty years or more now, and I'd like to keep it with me forever. All the while, these guys are asking me to put my right hand in this monster's mouth. This fish is huge. This is Moby Dick, the catfish.

When the guys asked me, "Did he bite you?" I had to tell the truth, "No, he scared me. I could block the opening, but that's all I can do is block."

In two hours, these guys caught five or six catfish, each weighing more than fifteen pounds. That's sixty to eighty pounds of catfish, enough to feed all of them and their families. The youngest of them held all those catfish up on a rope out of the water. They reached from the ground to a grown man's waist. They were that big—long and heavy.

A big mess of catfish.

William Bartram's drawing of a snapping turtle.

Because this shoot all took place right by the river bank, Doug took the camera on land to get tight shots. The grabblers were facing him and their faces made for great reaction shots. Since they were reaching in with their right arms, their faces were mostly above water. We got a few aqua-cam shots underwater, too.

With Doug on the land, we could see the bright-eyed, sixteen-year-old boy's face, while his hand was being chewed upon. "I got him!" the boy said . . . "Ouuch!" (Laughter) As the fish chewed on his hand, he made a series of grimaces. His kinfolk egged him on, "You got him?" they asked. He would nod, then, make a pained facial expression as the big catfish gnawed on his knuckle. There would be a chorus of catcalls and laughter, then, "That's fun isn't it?" The boy started to shake his head, as the fish bit him again. "You got him?" "Who's got who?" Ha! This fellow just kept nodding his head up and down, right and left and emitting a series of sounds. Some were "ah-hugh" for "yes." Some were "no" grunts. Some were loud "Ow's!"

It was the funniest six minutes of video I've ever seen. Doug captured his reactions perfectly. The trouble was our entire show only lasts three minutes and forty seconds, so we could only use a little of the footage.

For years afterwards, occasionally, I'd see one of George's nephews in Lowe's where he works in Knoxville. This way we kept up a little with all the clan. At a festival or outdoor event recently, perhaps fifteen years after "Grabblin" was shot, I heard about George and his boys, again. Our sixteen-year-old star has a family of his own now, and likes to take others out, grabbling, like his uncles before him. He's passing along his knowledge of this crazy adventure sport, and having fun doing it.

On land, finally, at the end of the day's shoot, while we helped load the gear and strapped the boats to the trailers, we were about to say our goodbyes when George approached us. Serious as a heart attack, George, with a broad smile, invited us to go with him to look for snapping turtles! We thought he was kidding.

Searching for Snappers

"When you reach your hand into a snapping turtle's hole, you just have to remember to keep your fingers together, Bill," George explained, while showing how you don't separate your fingers.

"If you put your hand in there and open your fingers, you know, split them apart where he can get you between your fingers . . . well, you don't want that."

No, I don't want that. I don't want that at all! Isn't a snapping turtle supposed to be able to hold on until it thunders? It rarely thunders around here; do you realize that? It rarely thunders at all!

This time, we were after snapping turtles of the ten-to-twelve-pound variety. George took us to every creek in Monroe County. We sloshed around in muddy water up to our waists for about six hours. We were in the snakiest places I've ever seen. I asked George what happens when you put your hand into a snake hole. "Aw, Bill," he said with a straight face, shaking his head. "We leave them. We don't eat them."

We just kept reaching under banks in dark creeks, light creeks, under big roots, anywhere a ten-pound snapping turtle could hide. According to George, when you reach into that snapper's hole, if you keep your fingers together and he snaps at you, there's nothing for him to get a hold of. "You just angle your hand up a bit to the roof of the hole. Then, begin to feel your way to the back, or as far as you can reach. Then, you either grab him by the tail and pull him out backwards, or feeling your way, grab him on the other side of the shell by the neck. But be careful, that's where his head will be. And just jerk him out of there!" Try that!

It's a thrill, I'll tell you. We felt around places and crevices in creeks on farms where no one has ever been, where briars and trees and honeysuckle and wild growth cover both sides of a creek, where it's so thick no one has even seen the creek. It was wild and mysterious, terribly beautiful. Doug had the aquacam. With his waders on, he just floated the camera everywhere we went. It was like that book *Green Mansions*—a world different from any yet seen, at least by me.

We stopped and ate our fill of ripe mulberries from a tree George found. Huge berries. I had no idea mulberries were so big. Ripe ones are as big as quarters, and tastier than ripe raspberries.

Worn out, by 4:00, we finally started catching some turtles. First, we caught a few painted turtles, little ones that would fit into your hand. Then, sloshing upstream in Sweetwater Creek, we came to a rushing pool below a little waterfall.

The splashing and noise coming from just below the falls startled us at first. It was carp rooting around. Then, just like he said he would, George yanked a ten pound snapping turtle out from under the bank. He was fighting it, yanking against some faster running water. It was below a shelf, but he had that big snapping turtle firmly by the tail, all right!

It was fierce looking and mad when he came out of there. We took more video of the turtle, and they dropped him into a burlap sack and took him home to eat. Turtle is a fine wild meat to eat. We've had some before. Cleaning the turtle took hours. It was hard to get the shell off, but the meat was great.

At parting, in true East Tennessee fashion, most folks will invite you to "Come back and set a spell!" or they might say, "Come back to see us!" And they mean it. Sometimes they'll invite you to just "Come see us, you hear?"

With George and the boys, we remember driving off. It was the end of a long day. The sun was setting, we could see them there. And as sincerely as a happy prayer, we could hear them say as they stood there waving, "Don't forget to check for leeches!"

A typical snapping turtle.

Tony Thomas, Charlie McCarroll, and Bobby Fulcher perform at "Gathering of Friends."

CHAPTER 14

Out of the Ordinary

"Rolle Holle Marbles"

There are special stories, because there are special people. Here are a few that came our way.

Folks around Bell County, Kentucky, and Clay County, Tennessee, just happen to be very, very good at something unusual. They are some of the best marble players in the world, but nobody knew anything about it. They play a game called "rolle holle," pronounced "rolley hole."

Above Dale Hollow Lake, folks aren't fanatics about baseball or basketball. They don't have fields, courts, or basketball goals everywhere. When they take breaks at their factory jobs, they don't play poker, hearts, or other card games. They shoot marbles, young and old. At home, they go out back to their yards and shoot marbles. And they do it better than anyone in the world, at least, that's what Bobby Fulcher thought, and he set out to prove it.

Rolle holle marbles is played on a court, called a yard. It's actually a sandy twenty-by-forty-foot flat rectangle. At first glance, it looks a little like a croquet-yard without any grass, with three little holes, each a little bigger than a marble, spread out across the yard. Some courts have lights, and games go long into the night, just like basketball.

This is the game that folks have played for a hundred years, or more. They use hand-made stone marbles that have been passed down for generations. Over time, these players have gotten very good at this game, extremely good. "Knuckle down," you'll hear 'em shout. It's what they do and what they've always done.

State Folklorist Bobby Fulcher wondered how good they really were, so, he hosted a competition, a tournament. Then, the eight best players would compete across the ocean at the International Marble Championships at Tinsley Green, England.

It was a wild idea, and to many Clay County folks it seemed a mite highfalutin, and even though many of the great players shied away from the tournament, not all of them did. It didn't make "no never-mind" to them. They just liked to shoot marbles. Plenty of good players turned out, including Jack and Junior, and Travis Cherry, and some others.

After all, this was to make the team for the worldwide competition. Teams from France, Australia, Germany, teams from all over the world would be there, including another American team fully sponsored by Marble Kings, the makers of glass marbles.

McClerren Marble Yard kids tournament.

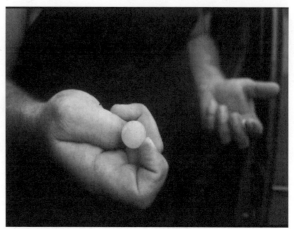

Close up shot showing the marble grip of Russel Collins.

These were mighty big steps for a little country team to take. How would they fare in the courtly world of big-time marble competition? Playing in windbreakers provided by the sponsoring factory, Bobby scrounged up enough state folklore funds for food and transportation. They wore overalls and tennis shoes, and stood tall against fully-uniformed competition.

When they asked Junior if he'd ever been across the ocean on a plane before, he said, "Heck, I just barely have been across the bridge!" Eight players made the trip, and Bobby conceded that some of the best players shied away from the competition. When asked why, Bobby explained, "They just don't show out! It's not the Clay County way."

Adapting their sprawling rolle holle game to the strict confines of English rules, they had to play in a tight eight-foot circle, where fifty blue marbles are knocked out of the circle, instead of longer shots into three tiny holes. They adapted well to this new game, and against highly supported, worldwide competition, only lost once.

They won eleven games, against all comers. When they arrived back home to the Nashville airport, and exited their plane, they were all wearing their championship medals, and they carried five or six four-foot-high trophies.

Over home, in Clay County, they still talk about that one rainy day in Tinsley Green, England, when our rolle holle marble players were crowned World Champions! They are Russel Collins, Travis Cherry, Bobby Dyer, Wayne Rhoton, Ron Branstetter, and Captain Jack Tinsley. They ARE the very best marble players in the world, and they've got the memories and the hardware to prove it.

Russel Collins competing at Tinsley Green, England in the World Marble Championships.

Out of the Ordinary

Porter School Women's Basketball State Championship Team.

Porter cars decorated for State Championship Tournament.

Porter gymnasium decorated for tournament fever.

Porter High Girls Basketball

Porter High School is in Blount County, or rather, it was. Today, it's a middle school, located in what was an agricultural area, the Wildwood Community. Porter High School was once a girls' basketball powerhouse. It wasn't big, though. In the 1960s, the entire school had two hundred and seventy-five students in twelve grades.

It was the time when women's basketball was played as a half-court game. You may remember; forwards were the only ones that could shoot the ball. Guards controlled the other team's forwards, and the ball was taken out at half court. Around 1973, or so, as a result of a Title IX court case, the women's half-court game ended. Prior to that time, Porter High School had a girls' basketball team, all right. And, oh, what a team it was!

Their coach, Galen Johnson, and Porter High School set standards and records, some of which will never be broken. In one twenty-year stretch, Porter High averaged twenty-eight wins a year. In one twelve-year stretch during that time, they won three State Championships, one second, and two third places. "That's six times in the money in twelve years. That's pretty good," Galen Johnson said to us, proudly.

This was in a time before classification, when you had to play everybody. There were no divisions, then. No AAA or 4A schools. Little schools like Porter had to play the giant schools like Chattanooga City and Memphis Melrose, with twenty-three hundred students in three or four grades.

There was only one state tournament, in which five hundred and seventy-one high schools competed. Blount County, Tennessee, was a hotbed for world-class women's basketball. Teams like Everett, Townsend, and Lanier provided Porter stiff competition, but Porter had the Rogers sisters.

To tell you how good at basketball they really were; during the 1960s, the United States Women's Olympic Basketball starting five included two players from Porter High: eight-time all-American Doris Rogers, and her sister, Marie.

This was a time before women were given scholarships. They couldn't earn scholarships or even attend college to play basketball like the boys. Galen Johnson's daughter, Stephanie Johnson Thompson, as an example, averaged thirty-six points a game for her entire four-year high school women's basketball playing career! She scored over three thousand points in high school; but, such a fantastic player couldn't play scholarship ball in college. There were no scholarships. She, and many others, played on intramural teams, if they played at all.

University of Tennessee Women's Basketball Coach, Pat Head Summitt, explained that when she took over the intramural team at U.T., and during her first years of coaching, she had a total of $3,000 in scholarship money for the entire women's basketball program. And U.T., it turned out, was one of the more progressive teams in the country.

"I could provide a thousand dollar scholarship to three players. That's all I had," Pat told us. "We played teams like Middle Tennessee State and Rock Hill, South Carolina, so we didn't have to spend the night. We couldn't afford it. We traveled in a van, the entire team packed in together. If we did spend the night, we slept five and six together. There wasn't any money for women's athletics then."

Today, Coach Pat Summitt is regarded as the greatest basketball coach who ever lived. Tennessee Women's Basketball is world class. Folks will tell you in Blount County that a great deal of the success is built on the earlier achievements of schools like Porter and Everett. Their fans, enthusiasm for the sport, and great players, provided a solid foundation for the success Women's Basketball experiences in our region today.

One more thing: The women's state scoring records that Porter High players hold will never be broken. The top three players, the all-time leading scorers in women's basketball, are Porter High School's Doris Rogers (3550 points), Marie Rogers (3547 points), and Stephanie Johnson Thompson (3490 points). Now that the half-court game is history, these amazing records will stand forever.

The Poet of Grundy County

Beersheba Springs in Grundy County, Tennessee is located on the other side of Sequatchie Valley, near the middle of the Cumberland Plateau. It was there that I once heard the historian of Grundy County say that Grundy County forever will be remembered for one thing, "It's the home of the poet, Leonard Tate."

This poem by Leonard Leon Tate, Poet Laureate of Grundy County, is one of my favorite all-time writings. The gentle poet was born 1912 in Beersheba Springs and died seventy-seven years later, in the same place. We were fortunate to meet him and hear him read this poem. He was so shy, though, he asked us not to record him reading it. Instead, we shot video of his beloved Beersheba Springs. The poem is called, "Mountain People."

Mountain People

We are mountain people.
We are a boorish set, they tell us —
Hard bitten, coarse of feature and of speech,
Shallow and brawling as the mountain streams.

All my life I have wanted to tell them:
That we are mountain people,
That mountain streams have pools
    of deep quietness
And that beneath the sandstone of our hills
There is granite.

Inez and Earl Adams at home in Cades Cove.

The Bond between Our Subjects and the Crew

Video tape recording isn't just for today; it's forever. You don't just shoot something for today, and then do it better tomorrow. It doesn't work like that. If you make mistakes, you can't just fix them. In TV documentary style, *Heartlanding*, you have one chance to do the story. You better get it right, because usually it's the only chance you get.

This is certainly true more times than not. I remember a revenuer we featured. Red was his name. We never did another story about the revenuer. It wasn't necessary. He was the real deal. What more could you ask for? What more is there than real?

If you choose to do a story on a country vet, you'd best talk to Doc Butler, an amazing veterinarian, who all the other country vets revered and respected. The same was true for quilters, or any other craft, talent, or "old method." In 1984, we met Opal Hatmaker of Clinton and did a good story with her. She was a great quilter.

At the same time, these *Heartland* subjects went out of their way to be kind to us. Often, they fed us, worked with our schedules, and invited us into their homes. It wasn't the other way around. They were generous, kind, and sincere.

It's a key, unwritten, and rarely talked about thing: the bond that existed between us and our television subjects. It was an unspoken agreement. We'd never make anyone look bad, stupid, or show them without respect. We tried never to make fun of anyone, except ourselves, even when people did some crazy stuff that we happened to catch on camera. We tried not to use it unless we could make fun of ourselves, too.

Once a guy was showing off some twenty-five-hundred-pound oxen. He was driving them from point A to point B, when they reared up and took off. Now, when oxen want to take off, there's no way anyone's going to stop them. When we caught up to them, they jerked and knocked this man's dentures clean out of his mouth.

The camera caught him reaching down and putting his teeth back in his mouth. It was pretty wild looking, but we didn't use it because it was a little too goofy. It wasn't worth it to double-cross a subject for a cheap laugh. Now, we've never been against cheap laughs. Hey, we're all about cheap laughs; just not at the expense of a *Heartland* subject.

There's a line we tried not to cross. We tried to treat people with respect. We wanted to show character and pride in the region and its people, not to make fun of them.

In a very real sense, we are responsible for our portrayal of these good people. We owe it to them, their families, their descendants, their neighbors to celebrate their lives and talents. We always told people, "If you don't look good, we don't look good." We believe that.

And boy did that lay heavy on us. In the cutthroat world of TV, with deadlines, egos, personal pride, budgets, and personnel restrictions, it was tough to live up to our own standards. It was difficult at times to keep our word to someone. There were a thousand things out of our control; but if we said something, or made a commitment, we tried to live up to it. That's it.

Living up to our own standards and acceptable levels of quality was not easy. Steve set the bar high. We had to work harder than we thought we could many times. We had to rewrite scripts, sometimes reshoot something. Often we were sent back to do more.

That was the case with Maynard Ledbetter's story, "The Homecoming," that first year. We had to go back, and then go back again with Maynard to Cades Cove. That's why, if you look closely, you'll see Maynard has on a different colored shirt in different scenes in the same show. Maynard always wore overalls, but his shirt magically changes colors.

Sometimes, particularly at the beginning, we just didn't know what else a show needed, or how to make it better. Steve checked our scripts for decades. Writers and producers met often. We added copy, rewrote endings, whatever it took to make it better.

That was the question: Is there anything else we can do to make it better? If the answer finally was

Quilter, Opal Hatmaker and me at *Heartland* on a hilltop.

Alcoa's Fred Brown, the Holly Man.

"no," then we would go to editing. It was asked in editing too. Does anyone have any ideas to make it better? If something bothered any of us, we brought it up. We worked well together. Everybody went through it, working tremendously hard, often long into the night.

How could we settle for anything less than our best, when our subjects didn't? That was another reason we went the extra mile. The way we worked evolved, and changed over time, but how we worked stayed fairly consistent. We worked hard because we could, and we loved doing it. It was always our subjects and their contributions that served as examples. It pushed us to do our best. "The Holly Man" is a good example of that.

The Holly Man

We were shooting a story in Alcoa called "The Holly Man," featuring a wonderful, gentle man who worked as a recruiter for the University of Tennessee, College of Engineering.

He traveled to many southern states for the university. His hobby, as he traveled from school to school, was to collect hollies. I believe the Latin name for holly is "Ilex." He found and relocated dozens of hollies: "ilex Teleflora," or "ilex Cornus," or something like that.

We called him the "Holly Man" and named the story after him. We visited his mother's modest home in Alcoa where he planted and grew all his many plants over the years.

He had assembled an enormous collection. He had holly trees, shrubs, plants, and bushes. I never knew so many existed in the world. His name was Fred Brown, an amazing man. He had been an assistant to Dr. George Washington Carver at Tuskegee. He learned to fly with the second or third wave of the Tuskegee Airmen. He also met and visited with poet Robert Frost at his farm. I remember him telling us stories about that.

Mr. Brown was an older man, in his seventies. It was a long, hot, lazy summer's day that we spent with him, a wonderful day that I'll never forget. We dug holes. He showed us how to plant holly shrubs and replant them. He used sphagnum moss, and demonstrated how to make cuttings, so that new plants would take root. We worked all day out in the hot sun and through it all he was happy, kind, generous and clever.

Fred was always concerned with wildlife habitat and creating wild places in his yard. He said, "Americans love to cut their grass, mow it just as close to the ground as they can. Skin it!"

Fred Brown was a great human being. At the end of the day, after we'd said goodbye and thank you, and loaded everything in the trusty *Heartland* truck, for some reason, I had to run back into his small, modest home. I'd forgotten something. When I knocked quickly and then ran back in, I surprised him. He surprised me too, when I saw him in his undershirt.

He was in the middle of the living room with an oxygen mask strapped around his head. His wife, or a neighbor friend, was assisting him with a breathing apparatus connected to an oxygen tank. The tank was next to him, and the woman was helping him take one breath after another, slow, deep important breaths, as if his life depended on this procedure; because it did.

When I came back into the room, he smiled at me. I picked up something, waved at him, and then ran out and got into the truck. It would be a

cruel understatement to say the Holly Man went out of his way to help us that day. Hell, he probably put his own health in danger by sharing his knowledge with us in that heat.

We'd worked hard, and he never once complained or asked for a moment's break. He carried little trees from one place to another and then did it again for the camera. He planted, he dug; he never once hesitated. I wish we'd known he was ill, but we didn't. We worked him too hard, and kept saying, "Could you please carry this or move that for the camera?"

He did this for OUR sake, not his. These people, our subjects, our *Heartland* friends, they

Black Will Walker and Old Barry, his ox.

Heartland Staff around 1999: Doug, Bill, Linda, Bill Archer and Amy Palmer, and Steve.

didn't need us. We needed them. We owe them our careers, our livelihoods, whatever we have in this business. That's why it was okay if we had to work a Saturday or Sunday to improve the product, even a little bit. It was a tremendous responsibility to work on *The Heartland Series,* and we knew it. We were lucky.

We were invited to a thousand birthday parties, church luncheons, pot luck suppers, baptisms, weddings, christenings, and funerals. We attended the ones we could. The *Heartland* people were not just our subjects. They were our friends. You do things for your friends, and they do things for you. That's why they're your friends.

CHAPTER 15

The Legend of Jonathan Swift's Lost Silver Mine

Swift and Timberlake

My two favorite stories are epic eighteenth-century tales that happened here in East Tennessee—"The Legend of Jonathan Swift's Lost Silver Mine," and "The Memoirs and Journey of Lt. Henry Timberlake."

The Heartland Series produced both of them, but in different ways. We made a gallant attempt to shoot "Swift" as a full reenactment. "Timberlake's Journey," we did as a history tale with Dr. Jefferson Chapman of the McClung Museum. We told the story, but did not use actors or recreate it. Both would make excellent screenplays and great films.

They have much in common. Each is set in the second half of the eighteenth century. Both deal with exploration and journeys into the newly discovered dark reaches of early Colonial America, particularly, East Tennessee. Native Americans figure in both tales, but more so in Timberlake's.

In both stories, our hero grows from a tenderfoot into a seasoned adventurer. They're set in pre-revolutionary America, amidst history in the making. The stories play out at the exact moment of first European contact. The time period and place are the real stars of the story. The drama is the result of the clash of cultures: European versus the Native Americans. The setting is 1760. Throw in the founding of a nation and the birth of new world government in America, and you have a very exciting old-fashioned family epic adventure on a grand scale.

The participating nations are the Cherokees, the British, and American colonial pioneers and early settlers in what became Tennessee.

The Treasure Hunters

History is fascinating, but as drama sometimes it can be a little boring. What *The Heartland Series* always tried to do in its storytelling was to spruce up the slow parts with the visual sweep of the story, the atmosphere, and the place; that is, showcase the natural world and the stunning beauty of our setting.

True history may have drama, tragedy, comedy, heartbreak, heroism, romance, and adventure, but if it's not portrayed, packaged imaginatively,

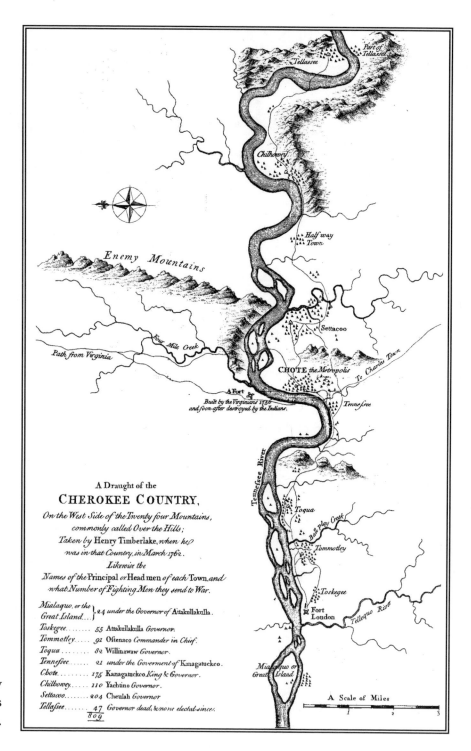

1760 map drawn by Lt. Henry Timberlake showing villages along the Little Tennessee River.

and communicated, you have nothing. Your story falls on deaf ears. One of Doug's favorite quotes from The Man Who Shot Liberty Valance is, "If the legend is better than the truth, print the legend." There's also another saying we try to remember: "Never let the facts get in the way of good TV!"

In 1987, our friends, Mike Steely and his rambling buddy, Roy Price of Jellico, first introduced us to the legend of Jonathan Swift's lost silver mine with such passion that we were immediately smitten with it and wanted to tell the tale, to shoot the story. The question of course was how? Holy mackerel, it's a full-blown movie! We do a three-and-a half-minute local TV show. How are we going to do a monstrous shoot with horses, actors, costumes, Native Americans, and props?

To help us "see" the production, Mike Steely and Roy Price took us to the wild edges of the Kentucky border and showed us huge stone arches and a spectacular rocky landscape, a possible great location for Swift's men to work the treasure. It's a tale requiring tremendous visual power.

It was such a remote location, but if we could get our actors, horses, and crew there, it could work.

Budget for Swift

The more we learned about the story, the more fascinating it became. We had the will, and the energy; we had to translate that into money. We just didn't have much money for the production. The challenge was to tell a great story, to produce an epic show without an epic budget. Counting costumes, lunch for the cast and crew, gas money, and paid actors, we may have spent $450. Because

Dr. Jefferson Chapman of the McClung Museum.

we also did another episode on "Treasure Hunting" around the Swift tale, we were able to make it affordable. Two shows for the price of one, you might say.

Roy Price and Mike Steely introduced us to Michael Paul Henson, the great historian, author, and some say, promoter of this tale. It is, after all, the "legend" of Jonathan Swift's lost silver mine. The very fact that it may be bunk, a lie, a legend, makes the entire story that much more attractive. At least, it did for us.

When we met Michael Paul Henson in Jellico, it was at the treasure hunters' promotion where people were selling books. It was a festival for treasure hunters, guys with metal detectors looking for silver, gold—treasure.

Michael Paul Henson was telling us about

Confused Roy Price at carved rock.

Roy Price, Jim Whidby, Mike Steely.

Swift, when he asked, "Do you know what mankind's two most powerful emotions are? What drives us like no other?" I was thinking love and pride, or perhaps, desire and fame. Before I could respond he said as confidently as a preacher, or St. Peter at the pearly gates, "Hope and greed—that's at the basis of all man's desires, all his actions."

According to Michael Paul Henson, these two emotions are the life force behind the legend of Jonathan Swift's lost silver mine.

[144]   Appalachian Tales & Heartland Adventures

The Legend of Jonathan Swift's Lost Silver Mine

Sometime around the late 1740s or 1750s there lived in Colonial Virginia, around the seafaring port towns and the docks of Norfolk, a struggling two-bit sea merchant named Jonathan Swift. One day, he stumbled upon a dying man in the street by the name of George Monday.

For some reason, perhaps just being charitable by nature, Swift took Monday in and nursed him back to health. As Monday's health improved, their trust and friendship grew and Monday related to Swift this fantastic tale of being captured and forced as a slave to work the silver mines by Indians. It happened while his family was hunting in the forested lands of Kentucky, and what is now Southwestern Virginia and Northeast Tennessee.

Monday told Swift that as a boy his brother had given him a torch and sent him into a cave after a wounded bear. That's where Monday first saw the silver. But, while inside the cave, Monday's brothers and father were attacked and killed by Shawnee Indians. Monday was captured and for years forced to work as a slave in the Indian silver mines.

Later, he escaped and made his way back toward the coast where Swift found him in his bedraggled state. Over the next years, Swift and Monday planned and executed a series of forays and expeditions into the wilds of Virginia, even following maps and existing trails out of Ft. Pitt into the western country.

Sometime in the early 1760s, following the Big Sandy River, they arrived near the place where a rock looks like a turtle. They traveled by the "seeing-eye rock," and other such signs and marks, carvings left by Monday when he made his original escape, so that he could find his way back to the treasure.

French and Indian War.

After searching a particular location for three days, Monday found the lost Indian silver mine. During the next six to eight years, Monday and Swift returned each season to mine their treasure. They brought with them silversmiths and counterfeiters from Barbados. At the same time, Swift's merchant fleet expanded and his fortune grew to include an entire array of more than a dozen seagoing vessels. This information is documented and available in records.

Sometime around 1768 with the Indian Wars raging, Swift and Monday, their men and operations, were attacked on the frontier. Under fire, they quickly buried their casks of ingots and treasure under a large overhanging rock, which they

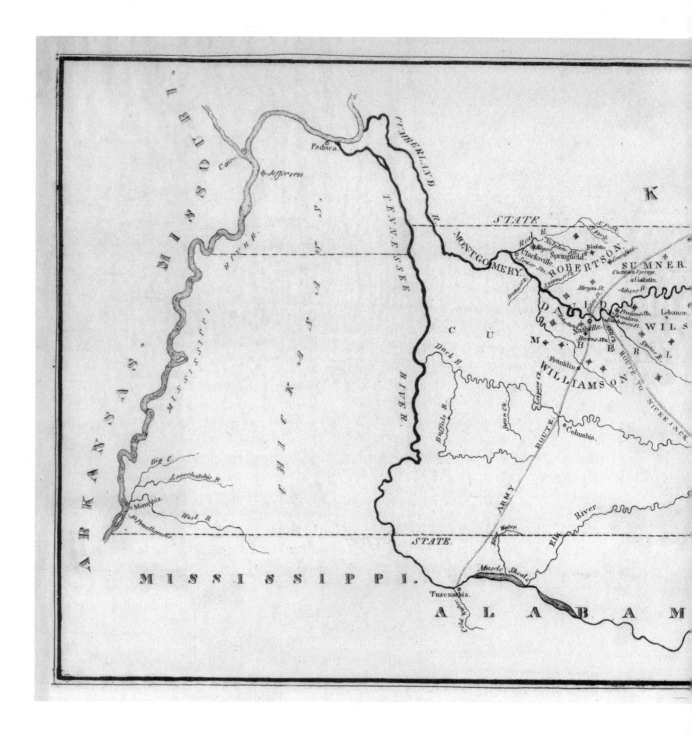

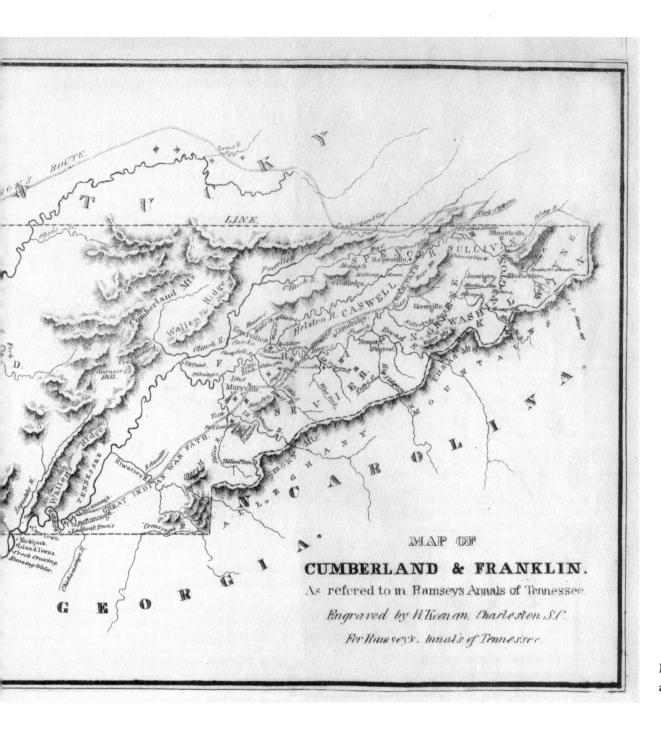

Map of Cumberland and Franklin.

Jim Claborn and Bill Archer.

The Shooting of Swift's Silver Mine

The first person record left from Swift's journal, with some rewriting, would serve as our script. Jonathan Swift would tell his own story.

We had three locations, at least, picked out, with a horse or two waiting for us, even some Native Americans. We bought lunch for everybody. Most had their own pre-revolutionary frontier costumes.

The *Heartland* players were assembled: Jimmy Claborn played Swift. Teacher, writer, actor, and scholar; Jimmy's best known as a storyteller. He's also an authority on Davy Crockett. He has helped and worked with us for twenty-five years, and is one of our best friends!

Rick Stroud, who is always inventive and wonderful as an actor and prop maker, came down from Morristown with Jimmy. There's always room in any shoot for Rick. We'd recently shot a great story called "The Sharpshooter." It featured Bill Blackburn, unquestionably the greatest marksman I've seen. Sadly, Bill died suddenly some time ago. However, Bill's two assistants volunteered to help on the Swift shoot. One had a full, thick beard; a giant of a man, perhaps six foot four inches and two hundred and fifty pounds. The other was a great actor. He looked just like we'd pictured George Monday to look—scraggly beard, thin, with a deep voice. When he said, "Silver! Just like I told you!" it sent shivers down your spine.

That's what was great about working with these guys. They all had their own gear, including long rifles of the period. So, instead of renting costumes, we paid the actors gas mileage and a small fee.

We had a good young actor playing Monday as

marked by laying stone crosshairs over it. Further, they marked the stones and left carvings so that they could find it again.

Upon Swift's return to England, he was imprisoned unjustly and languished for ten years. Blinded, he returned to America but never found Monday or any of his men ever again.

A journal he wrote was reportedly left to a Bean Station woman. In it was a map that supposedly gave the location of the silver mine. Swift wandered America blind, continuing to search for his treasure, but he never found it. His final comment, left in his journal, was this: "Boys, never quit searching for it. It's the richest thing I ever saw."

I don't really know whether Jonathan's Swift's lost silver mine exists or not, but it's fascinating to think that it might.

a boy, with my son, Jack, as his brother. We shot Jack handing young Monday the torch, and telling him to "Go get that bear!" It was great having Jack on the shoot.

It was fast and wild. Driving toward Jellico at 9:00 a.m. in the mountains, we saw the fog in the lowland valleys. Quickly, we stopped the car, grabbed the camera and two nearby actors and sent them straight out toward the sunrise with the mountains all around them. It was the perfect opening shot for the line, "We headed out from Ft. Pitt toward the western lands." Jumping back in the car, we drove to the next location.

"The Indian wars were raging," was a little tough to shoot because we only had two Indians, young ones at that. So what we did was to shoot over the shoulder of one as he looked around a tree. Then we could shoot again, and see him, as he moved through the forest watching Swift and his men. Doug made it work. We got good audio of the Native Americans attacking by having all of us yell!

We used a lot of POV (point of view) shots, and always had leaves and trees in the foreground. This created the illusion of dense forests, intrigue, and Swift's men being followed, etc.

We had two pieces of silver, ingots borrowed from a jeweler. An overhanging rock worked as the cave. Swift looked up above the camera in the silver mine and said: "We're rich, Monday." They reached up and Monday picked something out of the air, and said, "Silver! Just like I told you." We cut tight as he opened his hand to reveal the silver ingots. He showed it to Swift. It was just some melted silver, but it worked.

Since we didn't have many Indians, we couldn't show them attacking. So, we shot scenes of white men defending with their guns blazing while fend-

Steely's arrowhead made of silver.

ing off arrows. It worked even better! We shot different angles of Swift, Monday and their men under siege. Rick Stroud even managed to stick an arrow in his leg. It looked great as he was being dragged behind cover.

We stacked little bars of metal we'd brought for the counterfeiting sequence. Rick and the actors bit the coins, like they were real.

We were running out of time and light, so we grabbed Jimmy Claborn as Swift, pulled his shirt off, stretched him out in front of a rock, and used an old chain and lock to chain him, as if in prison.

Slowly the camera started to pan down, revealing his dirty hand, cut and bleeding from chiseling rock, and making signs. The shot continues, slowly revealing a grimacing, tortured Swift amidst the smoke. That was it.

I think either Amy Palmer or Ernie Ingle edited the Swift story, a great, epic adventure. It looked like *The Last of the Mohicans,* except it was three minutes and forty seconds long!

I always hoped we could one day shoot parts of "Swift" or "Timberlake" on location in Williamsburg, Virginia. Imagine seeing Swift finding a bedraggled Monday near death on the cobblestone street with costumed actors in the background.

I always dreamed we could go to Savannah, too, and shoot the England locations there. In Charleston, South Carolina, there is more than one exact replica of an eighteenth-century English sailing vessel. These great ships are used as seagoing schools, exact duplicates of the great ships that once crossed oceans.

Now they dock in Charleston harbor. It wouldn't take much to rent one and take it to sea for the day. We could bring our actors to Charleston and shoot "The Journey of Henry Timberlake"—with Chief Oostenaca and the young warrior, Attakullakulla, looking over the gunnels to a disappearing America; what a great shot! What a great story!

Perhaps, someday we'll get the chance.

CHAPTER 16

Where Story Ideas Come From

How did we find our stories? Why did we do some stories and not others? These are some of the questions we're asked. People, ideas, and places that fascinated us, more than likely also fascinated our audience. We tried to approach all our shows with child-like wonder.

When it came to picking shows, there were many things to consider. Could we do it, given the location, time required, and availability of help? Was it timely or not? Many stories were determined by season; like, plowing, water witching, training a workhorse, cutting wheat, planting by signs, tracking coyotes, fur trapping, or making molasses. Quickly, we found there's a right time and season for everything. It surprised us how much *The Heartland Series* evolved into working in harmony with the cycle of life in our region.

All of our stories were about 3:40 minutes long, and one story often led to another. The rule was, "You can't do a second story on the same subject, just because you can't cram it all into 3:40." It had to be two different ideas.

For instance, "The Legend of Jonathan Swift's Lost Silver Mine," led to the "Treasure Hunters," but "Treasure Hunters" was a different idea, not Part Two of the Swift story. We did three Hoop Creek Stories, about the wondrous community outside of Tazewell near Lone Mountain, but each was different. "The Fly Boys" led to featuring Ruth Thomas and the Ninety-Nines, a group of early female pioneer aviators. "Grabblin'," led to "Catching Snapping Turtles."

"Climbing LeConte" and "LeConte Lodge" is a pair of stories, too. Sometimes it takes as much energy and effort to do one story as two—like, "Winter on LeConte," and "A Cold Day."

In 1984, when we started, we called our Native American story before 1760 "Cherokee Dawn." Then, we picked up the story after 1760, which was shot mostly at Oconaluftee Village, and called it "Cherokee Zenith."

How One Story Leads to Another

Once, we were flying in an airplane with Farris Thomas, shooting aerials, and finishing up a story

[151]

Roscoe Stinnett.

"When I'd land, I had to unscrew my propeller and take it with me, or somebody would steal it!"

—Farris Thomas

about early pioneers of aviation. Our region was a hotbed for early fly boys and barnstorming pilots. Around here, people took off and landed airplanes in cow fields and pastures.

Many East Tennesseans saw their first airplane this way. Believe it or not, for a nickel or a quarter, some folks got their first airplane ride out of somebody's corn field.

Farris Thomas and Elmer Wood flew this way. They were pioneers of flight. Once we asked Farris if he was ever lost. "Ha," he laughed and said, "We was always lost. You get up above the clouds and you are lost! We didn't have any instruments, no dials on our dashboards that told us anything, we just flew. We had a compass, pretty haphazard, low tech, you might say. But, we were practical.

"I flew out of the old Sutherland Avenue airfield in Knoxville. Used the sun, the angles of the mountains for directions, followed the rivers. They were our roads. Ha. We were lost all the time. When I'd land, I had to unscrew my propeller and take it with me, or somebody would steal it!"

This day, we were flying over Blount County with Farris shooting aerial video for "The Fly Boys," which is what we called Farris's story. From the air, something caught our eye on the ground. We could barely see it nestled between two ridges. It appeared from the air to be a big green quilt!

When we finished the shoot, on the way home, we just drove over a ridge, and there, spread out before us, was Mr. Holder's watermelon patch. From the air, it looked like a green quilt, and it was full of big ripe watermelons. We thought, "Wow! What a great location for a story."

That Sunday after church in Harriman, I asked my father-in-law, Hal Jones, one of our chief consultants, a question. "Hal, did you ever steal a watermelon?" He looked at me surprised and said emphatically, "Naawww, No!" Then, with a twinkle in his eye, he smiled and said, "Well, I might-a took the heart out of one or two!" That's how the story began for "Watermelon Slippin," about three little boys who conspire to steal Mr. Holder's biggest watermelon.

By the way, Mr. Holder, it turned out, is Jennifer Holder's uncle. Jennifer is a good friend, and Vice-President in Public Relations at First Tennessee Bank, and helped often, particularly with an April Fools story about kangaroo dynamite!

That crazy show was where we moved the First Tennessee Bank building across the street to a vacated *News Sentinel* lot. It was orchestrated by a con man/architect and the inventor of kangaroo dynamite, portrayed wonderfully and coincidentally by Harry Wade. Appropriately, the story was called "The Move." It's a small world, the world of *Heartlanding*.

Most ideas came from people and were triggered by history, places, or even trees. We did ten stories on the types of trees and wood we have here in our region. We did stories on all the animals, many of the birds, fishes, mussels, rabbits, even an albino squirrel. You name it, if it's alive, we did a story about it—rockfish, sauger, darters, trout—we love doing stories about trout, but Steve made us quit!

Many story ideas came from letters, phone calls, and later, emails. People stopped us at grocery stores, football games, and church. "Hey, you ought to do a story about Uncle Fud. He knows a lot of history." The more times we heard about something, the better chance we'd have of figuring out if it was something we should do. We were slow, but finally, we'd get it!

In the early years of *Heartlanding*, we bought all the Foxfire books and used them as a sort of guide. They were full of great suggestions.

Tanning a Hide with Lukie Ballew

"This is hard work, Lukie."

"That's what you was put here for, Bill . . . is to work!"

We wanted to do a story on tanning a hide, and to feature the process of actually doing the tanning ourselves. It was 1987 and we were doing a lot of processing stories, "how to" shows. Somehow we'd heard about Lukie Ballew of Monroe County, who always said he was from the "red hills and knobs of Mon-roe County."

"Monroe," for your information is pronounced as two complete words with equal emphasis on each: Mon-Roe. And "Lukie," his name, was actually Luke. But, he always called himself "Lukie."

Talking to Lukie by phone, he wanted us to bring a bear skin to tan. Well, I didn't have one, and the prospects weren't good for me finding one, either. That's another thing about doing the *Series*: the raw materials. Getting the raw materials for an episode can be difficult. If you're doing "Opossums and Sweet Potatoes," you can't just go down to Food City and get your opossum. You have to find one and, usually, catch it.

The same thing holds true doing a story on tanning a hide. We needed something to tan, a skin. Lukie said, "Bring borax, saltpeter, and alum, three ingredients you can find in any country store."

Well, maybe the stores Lukie frequented, but not the ones in and around West Knoxville. It was difficult, but we found them. Now, we just needed hides.

Roscoe showing his firs, as Doug showcases *Heartland* gear, tripod, and recorder.

Tom Gheen was the best hunter in West Knoxville, everybody knew it. He volunteered to provide us a groundhog hide in order for us to have the raw materials for groundhog shoelaces that Lukie wanted to make. See how it all works together to do an episode?

Tom lived on Westland Drive right across the street from where West Valley School is now. At that time it was Tom's watermelon patch. That's where I asked him if it was good farm land and he smiled and said, "If you want to find a rock, you better bring it wichee!"

One day, on a Thursday, I got a call about 3:00 from Tom. He was excited. He'd trapped a groundhog in his watermelon field, and he wanted me to come get it. "It's a biggun, Bill."

So, I picked up my son Jack at school, and we went running across Tom's field. Tom started yanking at that groundhog, and finally, we got him

Where Story Ideas Come From

Alexis Magnotti set to edit Lukie in "Tanning a Hide."

out of there. He tied it to his barn, skinned it, and gave me the hide.

I snuck it into my freezer for a few days. It was half of what we needed—the groundhog shoelaces part. Now, all we needed was a bear hide to tan. I might as well be looking for a white buffalo!

I settled for a sheep hide, and that wasn't easy. It came from U.T. Agricultural Campus. "Yea," they said, "on Thursday night we've got a sheep to skin. If you help, you can have the hide." By 11:00 p.m. I was back home and pretty stinky, but I had my sheep hide. It, too, went in the freezer, unbeknownst to my wife.

It wasn't long before we were heading south on I-75 to Lukie's place near Niota. We had learned the hard way NOT to miss lunch, no matter what. So, we stopped at the Dinner Bell Restaurant in Lenoir City and ate "Uncle Fud and Aunt Suzie's Giant, Big-Time Breakfast for Hogs, Entire Families, and Gluttons," like us.

When we arrived sleepy at Lukie's house and opened the door, we found Lukie's bride had set a beautiful big table of food just for us. With sheepish smiles, we did what any TV crew would do. We sat down and ate again.

We finally got ready to work a little, though we really wanted to take a nap instead. Lukie was ready, though. We had skins, alum, borax, and saltpeter; and Lukie had the knowledge and will to show us how to do it. We were a great team this day.

Two days and sixteen hours later, after using a brick to scrub fat off the animal hides, I'd just about had enough of this fun. We made shoelaces by placing the groundhog skin in the top of a fifty-gallon oil drum, then covering it with ashes, and let it sit overnight. The next day all the hair was removed from the hide and Lukie just cut the leather skin into strips. Presto, change-o! We had shoelaces.

The sheep hide was a different animal, so to speak! We mixed the ingredients and sprinkled them on the hide, fur side down, and scrubbed the skin clean. The chemicals reacted with muscle power to grind the meat and fat away. In the sun, it was hot, hard, and slow going. It's one of those processes marked "for professionals only!" You DO NOT WANT TO TRY THIS AT HOME.

Late on the second day, with only an hour's work, or so, left, I'd had enough. Everything was shot, and I was beat. As my brick tumbled aimlessly from my raw, aching hand, I half cried, "Lukie, this sure is hard work."

Doug had the camera angled below him, so Doug was shooting up, looking at Lukie's face as he continued scrubbing away. He just smiled and said, "That's what you wuz put here for, Bill, is to woooorrk!"

We rinsed it, and half dried that hide in the sun. Washed and rinsed it, again. Lukie gave that hide to me. Today, I have it hanging on the second floor railing of my house/cabin home. Every time I see that hide, I think of Luke Ballew. It's hard to clean. Still, it's lasted for twenty-three years, and shows no sign of wearing out anytime soon. It was tanned the right way, which again, as usual, was the hard way!

Alexis Magnotti was the *Heartland* editor for Lukie's story. She was a great editor in a long list of great editors for the *Series*. Alexis was gifted, a joy to work with, but she didn't like Lukie.

Lukie Ballew and "Tanning Hides" was just not something Alexis was interested in. She loved all animals but especially cats, furry little kittens. Some of this, what we were doing, was less than appealing to Alexis, a Vassar graduate who was extremely smart! It came to a head, too, when I asked Lukie, "How long will it (the hide) last? How can you use it?"

"Aw Bill, it'll last forever. You can take your girlfriend or your wife, and a great big picnic basket full of lunch, to the mountains. Bring this hyere hide with you. Throw it out there on the ground when ya get to where yer a-goin', and just say, 'Spread that food, darlin'!' Ha!"

Now, I don't know that Lukie meant anything untoward by this or not, but Alexis, God bless her, did not take kindly to Lukie's remarks! That's an understatement.

It makes me laugh out loud today, twenty-three years later. I can hear her bemoaning his chauvinistic comments. "He didn't mean anything. He's over seventy years old!" I kept telling Alexis for days. "He's talking about a picnic, what's wrong with that?"

Stars of "Asses on Asses."

But she would have none of it. Lukie and "Tanning a Hide" just rubbed Alexis Magnotti, one of our great *Heartland* editors, the wrong way. "Spread that food, darlin'!" is something she didn't want to hear.

One more Alexis story—I'm telling it for the truth! We were working around Loudon with a group that rode mules at night and chased raccoons. It was a funny story about "Coon Hunting" on mules. Mules can run right up a mountain. They're as sure-footed as goats.

Well, this "Coon Hunting" tale was another story that didn't sit well with Alexis, you might say. I rode a mule with some great people, women included. We treed some coons. It was a good show. It was fun, too. But, Alexis always referred to that show as "Asses on Asses." I wonder why?

Why We Featured Some People and Not Others: Serendipity

Sure, many other people were just as deserving as some of the people we featured. Some were probably even more deserving. But, it wasn't about deserving. Some people were simply available. It was as simple as that, pure serendipity.

The same question could be asked about the stories in this book. Why have I included the World War II stories or Lukie Ballew's story? I don't know. Maybe it's just simply because if I don't tell them, nobody will.

I think the stories I've included are worth hearing, and telling again, and saving. They tell us something about who we are. These people and their stories are amazing to me. I'm lucky to have gotten to know them and so, skewed view or not, I'm telling them here for the truth.

Last of the Great Adventures

One idea Doug and I regret not doing is a video study of "All the Trails of Mt. LeConte in all seasons." We didn't think of it until late in our careers. To do it, to cover all seasons and all the trails, we figure it would take about twenty trips up LeConte.

I'm bringing this up because we didn't see this next one coming. Why we couldn't understand our physical limitations as we neared the end of our *Heartland* careers, I'll never know, but we didn't.

It probably has to do with pride, because pride is usually at the root of all my problems. It became painfully aware to us on "The Flint Mine" shoot, one of our greatest adventures. It was late in our careers to attempt such a physical shoot. I was fifty-five, and Doug was fifty-two. However, experience-wise it was a good time.

I've always been fascinated by archeology, and one night Dr. Charlie Faulkner invited us to attend a lecture by Dr. Jan Simek, Distinguished Professor of Science. We'd worked with Charlie on petroglyphs and cave art. He wanted us to hear Dr. Simek, who had been working on a fifty-thousand-year-old cave in France. It was fascinating.

Later, Dr. Simek became interim President of the University of Tennessee, but that night, he was a teacher and not an administrator, and introduced some interesting ideas to us.

Because of its limestone makeup, the Tennessee Valley is riddled with caves. We all knew this from exploring caves in our childhood. Dr. Faulkner and a few others had discovered cave drawings and paintings inside many of these caves. Carbon dating tells us they go back some three to five thousand years. Dr. Simek and others also discovered what appeared to be an ancient Native American flint mine which provided the raw materials for arrowheads, spears, stone tools, and such. The owners of the cave where the flint mine was located had granted permission to scientists to explore it.

We thought the project could look like a National Geographic special. We'd bring enough light into the cave to show actual exploration. This was around 1990. But there was a problem, a fly in the soup, as they say. The landowners didn't want a camera crew taking pictures, in spite of our assurances to never disclose the location. It looked like this story wasn't going to happen.

Fast forward fifteen years to 2005. Technology has improved remarkably. Doug's using a digital camera, and often shoots in High Definition. Battery packs have been replaced by portable LED lights. Everything is smaller, lighter, and more compact, but we're older, slower, and achier. It's

Dr. Jan Simek recording Alabama cliff art.

fifteen years after we *should* have done the story. Jan asks us again if we want to explore the flint mine, and we mistakenly say "Yes."

"The Flint Mine" turned out to be difficult and painful, certainly one of the most physical stories we ever attempted. This story smacked us in the face. It whipped our butts good! And we've been whipped before, but never this badly, or for this long. This is the shoot where the *Heartland* crew faced our mortality, and came up lacking! It wasn't a pretty picture. *Heartland* "hit the wall" and the wall won.

The plan was to spend the night on the Cumberland Plateau, rise early, cook, and eat hearty. We would pack lunch and hit the trail at first light. To do it, we had to get up at 4:30 a.m. and make it to the mouth of the cave by 10:30. That should enable us to make it back to the truck by dark.

Rob Adolfson was working in Detroit and flew back to Knoxville the night before, then drove two hours just to help us. Bill Archer was to run sound. Rob was to carry and set the lights in the cave, but Rob's plane was late, and he didn't get in till 11:00

We assembled at the river and hiked another mile. Finally, fairly exhausted, but still feisty, we arrived at the mouth of the cave on schedule. The cave has a great name, but we'll just call it Prometheus.

At that moment, it dawned on us that somewhere deep inside this cave there exists a Native American flint mine. After three thousand years, if we're lucky, we're going to see it. This really is "King Solomon's Mines," right here in this remote section of East Tennessee! All we have to do is follow the leader to see it. These cavers and scientists know what they're doing.

It was like *Journey to the Center of the Earth*. Prometheus had waterfalls and ravines where we dropped stones and couldn't hear them hit bottom. Once, we crossed a fifteen- to twenty-foot span by holding on to stalagmites and edging our way along the wall of the cave above a forty-foot drop. We handed our packs over to one another and then carefully crossed one at a time. It was slow going.

The cave was amazing. Often, the ceiling was out of sight. Sometimes we could walk upright. Sometimes we were bent over like coal miners. Walk, we did. And walk for nearly two miles inside that cave.

We all wore hard hats, an absolute necessity. By the time we got out of the cave, my ears were ringing from knocking my head into the side of rocks, cave walls, and stalactites. You can't see them; they sneak down from the ceiling, and then your head ricochets off them like in a pinball machine. Boing! Your brains are rattled because you've just crashed into a wall or ceiling secured to forty gazillion tons of rock and earth. It doesn't give even a little bit.

I wouldn't trade the experience of seeing the

At top: Doug, Jan, and me inside the Flint Mine, the Third unnamed cave.

Below Landry in a stupor in Third unnamed cave.

p.m. Then, he got lost and didn't arrive until nearly 2:00 a.m., so we didn't get much sleep.

There were three teams going into the mine: Dr. Simek and his archeology students, the cavers, and us. There were perhaps fifteen people on this shoot.

Things didn't go well from the start. In addition to Rob being late, as we started hiking out of the camp, a big copperhead snake startled us. It was beautiful, but it was dead. Was this an omen, "dead, like us," a precursor of what lay ahead?

We hiked about a mile to the edge of a gorge, then, dropped nearly a mile straight down to the river bank below with our forty-pound packs. The footing was difficult and steep. We couldn't sit back and slide down the mountain, our butts wouldn't reach the ground. Our packs were in the way. So, trying to slide down, a few of us flipped over face first. No problem! Just shake the leaves out of our ears and continue on down.

inside of that cave for anything, but I don't want to do it again! We stopped to shoot interviews, footage of waterfalls, climbing, walking. It just took a lot of time. Shooting video is slow anyway, and inside a dark cave it's much slower.

We shot the remains of three-thousand-year-old torches, and the scrapings of where torches were rubbed against five or six-foot ceilings in the cave. It leaves pieces of carbon that can be studied to tell the date of the material. What's amazing is the large number of people who must have gone this far underground and worked three thousand years ago. We had the latest twenty-first-century equipment, and it was difficult for us to get this far.

People explored here, found the flint, then, worked it a thousand years before Christ was born, and twenty-five hundred years before the first Europeans arrived on this continent. Unbelievable!

We followed along until the cave opened through a ceiling hole into what the cavers called the "heavens." There were a hundred similar openings, cracks in the walls that led nowhere, but this one led up into a room. Doug and I were the first ones through it with the lights and camera. It was only about two-and-a-half feet in diameter. Handing the equipment through the opening, we crawled through, connected the lights, and turned the switch.

You have to understand the thrill of this moment—not just for us, but for Dr. Simek and the cavers who found this sacred place. The ceiling was twenty feet high, and the room was fifty yards or more in length, tapering down at the far end into darkness. We could see the edge of the ceiling where it sloped down to two or three feet.

The lights revealed for the first time what had never been seen before. It was mesmerizing. There were little work stations, maybe twenty little piles of flint, two feet high, scattered around the room, absolute proof that people worked here three thousand years ago. It looked like they had just gotten up and left.

It was like a factory where grapefruit-size nodules of flint were worked in this space. Somehow the ancients figured out how to light this space and work there for hours at a time. The flint was broken apart, busted open with hammer stones, and the best pieces were carried out, according to Dr. Simek. We found drawings and cave art scraped into the walls: birds, spiders, and snakes. Unbelievably, we even saw tiny foot prints engraved forever into soft mud. They had remained undisturbed for thousands of years.

We finished shooting and started back out through the "rabbit hole" with a completely different feeling. There was a very respectful counte-

Seventh unnamed cave, Tennessee turkey petroglyph.

Doug shoots while I debate climbing the Chimneys in 2009 . . . or not.

Where Story Ideas Come From [159]

Petroglyph 2. Note dark places used as ancient footsteps. Actual foot prints were left.

zigzagged up the side of the gorge, like a switchback train line. We were scattered across a quarter mile section of the side of the mountain.

Everyone was trying to find an easier route, but there was none. We couldn't get any footing; we were so exhausted. We'd take three steps up and slide back down. It was frustrating and getting late. Darkness was coming. That's the only time in our entire twenty-five years of *Heartlanding* that I've ever seen Doug Mills give up. He just sat down and didn't move. After a sixteen-hour day hauling gear, hiking five miles, shooting the entire story, and then, to have to climb up a mountain face, it was just too much! He'd had enough. Me, too.

Doug sat quietly, without fanfare or fuss! When I reached where he was on the side of that mountain, he still hadn't moved. He mumbled something. Then, I heard him stammering to himself, as he waved ahead to the others, "GO AHEAD BOYS, SAVE YOURSELVES!"

Thankfully, with the help of the cavers and grad students, we made it out of there. Those sweet students, those tough soldiers, came back for us. They found us in pitiful shape and assisted by carrying our gear. It was our last twenty-hour *Heartland* day. It changed us. We had come face to face with the sad fact that we were not young anymore.

nance about us. Everyone realized how fortunate we were to have seen what we did. We were exhausted emotionally and, physically, we were well past tired. On the way out, we were running on fumes.

It took almost an hour and a half to reach the entrance to Prometheus, where we rested and drank what water we had left. To get back, we had to climb straight up. We couldn't, of course, so we

CHAPTER 17

A Gathering of Friends

"To everything there is a season, and a time to every purpose under heaven. A time to be born and a time to die; a time to plant and a time to reap that which is planted."

(Ecclesiastes, Chapter 3, Verse 2)

All good things come to an end. Perhaps, we remember them as good things because they came into existence, flourished, had their moment, faded, and were gone. We don't want to let go of good things, but that's the way of all life.

The Conclusion

The *Series* continued on after Steve Dean retired in 2004. Doug Mills, Sam Moore, a wonderful young editor who began as a *Heartland* intern from UT, and I—the *Heartland* staff, continued producing episodes, but the writing was on the wall. It wasn't just the economy, though. Doug and I, dare I say it, were getting older. We'd been doing the *Series* most of our adult lives.

It wasn't that we wanted the *Series* to end—it was simply we recognized it would come to an end eventually. There were many stories left to do, but we were now aware of our own *Heartland* mortality. We were on the downside of our *Heartland* careers and knew it. We'd begun thinking about legacy, and what we would do in our next life after *Heartland*. Professionally, we weren't actively looking for other jobs, but we were putting out feelers to see how we might make a living when the *Series* ended.

At the same time, our number of viewers and public recognition were never greater. More and more people were coming up to us every day and thanking us for the *Series*. They meant it, too. I remember a particular incident that occurred on a beautiful fall day in 2008. An older gentleman approaching a grocery store saw me, smiled, and came over to say hello.

I didn't know him, but I sensed he was a *Heartland* fan and thought I knew what he was going to say, but this was different. The gentleman took the time to cross the parking lot and came out of his way to see me. He looked me straight in the eye, put his hand gently on my shoulder, patted it, and then said, "You're a good man, Bill Landry. You're a good man."

That's it. Then, he turned and went back to his

Left: Joanne Woods and Linda Billman are caught on the stairs in 1987. Joanne went on to become Director of Network Operations, Scripps Network. *Right:* Sam Moore produced an episode on the only freshwater jellyfish in the world on Fontana Lake.

life, and I never saw him again. I don't know his name and can't remember what he looked like. I just remember what he said and that he meant it. He was sincerely thankful for *The Heartland Series*. It meant a lot to him.

No one has ever told me I was a good person before. I am touched by it and grateful. I know we did our best, and I'm pleased our work had value.

Financial Crash
Leads to the *Series* End

During these last few years we tried to do the stories we felt we should and needed to do. We wanted to make them count, to do them exceptionally well. I remember Steve's last story in 2004.

It was called, "The Discovery," one of my all-time favorites, and a great story with which to end a career at WBIR. It was a Christmas tale set during the "Trail of Tears."

Amy Anderson, our writer/producer, and Perrin, her husband, who also worked at the station for a time, had a baby. That's one reason Steve wrote "The Discovery." Amy, as it turned out, was our last *Heartland* producer. After her maternity leave, she retired. For the last five years, Doug Mills, Sam Moore, and I, continued to work without a writer/producer; we sort of went it alone.

Counting Steve, we had three different bosses during our last five years. For a time, we had Mathew as our executive producer. Then, around 2007, Julie Morris became our final boss. Sam Moore, our editor, began to carry more of the work load and producing responsibilities.

Sam is fastidious, creative, naturally inquisitive, and extremely competent. He's also brave, clean, and reverent! Mostly, he's committed to doing it well, a stickler for detail and depth. By 2007, he was about as good as it gets.

Julie was helpful and understanding in an awkward situation when she arrived. She was great at her job; we had a lot of fun, and worked well together.

We were starting to feel the lean times. Still we managed to do some great shows. Julie arranged this for us. Occasionally, Laura Armour or Linda Billman would work a week or so with us, just like old times. I always worked well with Laura, and over the years we've continued to work well together on many projects. It gave us a break, allowed for a vacation week, or just a chance to do a bigger, better episode.

One of the shows Linda wrote and produced featured Dr. Michael Birdwell and Dr. Calvin

Doug with Julie Morris, our final Heartland Executive Producer, at the Chimneys.

Laura Armour, then Laura Eubanks, writer/producer, in 1987 at WBIR.

Dickinson, historians and writers from Tennessee Technological University. The story was called "Bushwackers," and told the Upper Cumberland Plateau tale of murderers Tinker Dave Beaty and Champ Ferguson. They terrorized the region during the Civil War. It was a great story.

2007—When the Economy Went South

My final two-year contract ran through September 9, 2009. During this period, the television business everywhere was experiencing massive layoffs. Older employees were being offered early retirement packages.

Operations were being consolidated. The graphics department was dissolved at the station and the operation of master control was moved to a national, central location elsewhere. It seemed that everything in America was becoming more streamlined. Television was no exception. The business as we knew it would never be the same again.

Gannett Corporation, which had bought WBIR-TV, Channel 10, from Multimedia, owned many newspapers, including *USA Today*. They

WBIR Engineers: Ronnie Hall, Don Burggraff and Varnell Wolfenbarger around 1987.

A Gathering of Friends [163]

Here I am with John Rice Irwin and a smiling, Doug D. Mills. (The "D" is for danger).

Bill Landry, Steve Dean, and Jim Hart.

owned eight or so television stations as well, but the newspaper business was Gannett's bread and butter. Advertising revenue was at an all-time low. TV stations scrambled to survive. The ones that succeeded adapted the quickest to the new business paradigm.

Soon, the recession was in full swing. It was a sad time. Many long term employees and members of the Channel 10 family left the station. Some retired or left for other jobs and some, sadly, left with no job to go to. This was happening everywhere. Nearly every business in America was affected and the outlook was grim.

Near the end of 2008, Doug Mills, along with many other technical people, was offered a retirement package. Our long term sound man, Bill Archer, was caught up in this cutback and he retired. This occurred six-months or more before my contract was set to expire—with no chance of it being renewed. It was clear *The Heartland Series* was unceremoniously coming to an end. Nothing was announced officially; we just deduced it.

Somehow, however, Doug arranged to continue working through 2009, to finish out the work of the *Series*. He would continue at least until I was done, the first week of September.

As effective as our *Series* was locally, the decision was final. Since the financial problems were national and corporate, the decision stood. Even though we showed a profit, it was clear the *Series* couldn't survive with little or no support from upper management, at least, not in its current form. So, after twenty-five years of operations, *The Heartland Series* was ending. The only question was how it would happen.

The Party—The Legacy

WBIR's General Manager Jeff Lee and Julie invited Steve Dean out of retirement to participate in the final chapter of the *Series*. Steve had been crucial to the *Series*' creation and development. It was only appropriate that he and Julie together orchestrate its ending, our final act.

Their idea was to have a big party and invite everyone who helped and thank them. In that way, we could all celebrate the *Series:* not mourn it. It was a great idea, to go out in typical *Heartland* style.

This gathering would be a celebration of everything the *Series* stood for. It would be for the people featured in it, and their families; the audience, viewers, and fans; and, finally, those who worked on it: producers, writers, WBIR sales people, and management. Whew! What a guest list.

It would be just like our first *Heartland* Christmas at the Mountain View Hotel. Only this time we would invite everyone from twenty-five years of shows, nineteen hundred episodes. Steve contacted Elaine Mayer and her father John Rice Irwin to have the event at the Museum of Appalachia. Its grounds could handle the crowd.

Thematically, it seemed right, as many of our best stories were shot there. The Museum of Appalachia held many great memories for us. John Rice Irwin was, in a sense, our mentor. For twenty-five years, he helped, advised, answered questions, and allowed us to use the Museum as a location. He was gruff and he sure could be ornery, but he always said "yes" to us. You just never wanted to trade with him!

It was an enormous organizational effort. We'd met thousands of people over decades of doing stories. How could we invite everyone? What would they do when they got there? Like anybody throwing a party, there were concerns about attendance. Would anybody show up?

Meanwhile, the public's reaction to the end of the *Series* was building momentum. It was developing into a full-fledged brouhaha! Facebook was collecting thousands of signatures to save *Heartland*. People were writing letters to the general manager and the corporate offices trying to change the station's mind. It was a turbulent and tumultuous period.

Doug and I tried to make the best of a bad situation. We were losing our jobs, but we tried to be confident that things would work out. They always have. It was almost as if we felt this public effort to save the *Series* was wonderful, but there

Here I am with Mule Man, Joe Long, who helped us for decades.

A Gathering of Friends

Horse wrangler, Sam Tillery, aboard Red Bud provided horses and travel for us many times.

wasn't much anybody could do. It was much ado about nothing.

This rebirth of interest was strange though. A trust had been broken. It was a bit awkward, now. It was a little funny, like, crazy funny. We certainly didn't want this event, this party, to be something just simply concocted for promotion by the station—it was that in part, of course, and we knew it. But, if we were going to have this party, we were going to work extremely hard to make it as sincere and meaningful for our viewers and fans as possible.

Difficulties in Saying Good-bye

The reaction to the unfavorable announcement that the *Series* was ending was enormous. There was a public outcry. The audience, the viewers were angry. They felt betrayed and double-crossed by the station and the corporation they'd been supporting. Here was a TV program they liked and enjoyed for twenty-five years, and there would be no more stories. They didn't like that. They didn't understand it, and frankly, neither did we. We'd turned a twenty-seven percent profit, in 2008. It wasn't like the *Series* was unprofitable.

It was a confusing time. The public's reaction probably surprised the station; the size and sheer numbers of our audience following. It demonstrated the audience appreciation for the show, our work, and the fact the viewers cared about us. This bolstered our confidence, too, when we needed it. We'd been downsized, let go.

We tried to behave and enjoy ourselves at the same time. We tried to take care of our families and look after *Heartland*'s future. But, for the first time, these two goals were at odds with each other. One minute we were philosophical and melancholy, the next, angry, and frustrated. Like everybody else losing their jobs, we looked for somebody to blame.

We had talks and meetings with other stations. There was some interest to continue our work in another form. However, without the *Heartland* library, our history, and use of all the edited nineteen hundred episodes which belonged to WBIR, we would need to produce two shows a week at another station. Doug and I considered it, but it just didn't seem right this late in our careers. These offers and options helped our state of mind, even though we didn't pursue them.

Meanwhile, the party was going to happen. Julie had brought in extra folks in Promotions to help with it. So, there was a flurry of excitement and a whir of activity. We contacted and interviewed old friends and co-workers, people

we'd known for decades, but hadn't seen for a long time. We reminisced about shows, and years, and people. "The Gathering of Friends" was just that and nothing more. Wow! What a time. What a life.

A Gathering of Friends

We tried to personally invite as many people as we could to the party. We invited craftspeople, storytellers, musicians; Joe Long, the Mule Man, and Sammy Tillery, who provided much help with the horses.

We invited Bill Jones, known for his love of horses; Joan Wolf, who made us opossum and sweet potatoes; Jimmy Claborn, actor, writer, and friend, who co-wrote all our Crockett stories for twenty-five years; scientists, scholars, park rangers, Kim Delozier and Steve Moore, who we had worked with for all twenty-five years. And they came.

Everyone who appeared in a *Heartland* episode gathers for a huge photo.

Among the crowd of ten thousand, a young boy demonstrates his skill with an axe.

We invited scientists, whittlers, cooks, fishermen, herb doctors, quilters, trappers, everybody we could think of! For weeks we phoned people six hours a day.

The Promotions Department was smoking! Doug and I called all of our story contacts. Linda Billman, Laura, and many others did the same or called in names and numbers for us to call. At the same time, Julie and others worked out parking, scheduling, food, and everything else.

I can't begin to list who showed up. Thousands and thousands of people did. No, I didn't get to see and thank everybody, but I tried. When I arrived early at the Museum, heavy morning dew covered everything. Some people had camped out the night before.

At 7:00 a.m. Mike Witcher, the Channel 10 Weatherman, was standing in a field directing traffic. His pants were wet up to the knees from the dew. He didn't have to be there, but he wanted to help in some small way.

Russell Bivens, Larry Efler, Julie Morris, Kathy Woodson, Carson Hunt, Eric Fox, all these good friends from the station were there early. We were touched. It was that kind of a day. We were humbled and made grateful all day long. We didn't know how many people would show up but, by the end of the day, somewhere around ten thousand people had come by. I signed my name on hats, T-shirts, anything or anywhere anybody asked me. I did this for at least eleven hours.

Thinking back on it now, it happened so fast. The day went by like lightning, a blur of seeing so many hot, smiling faces. I remember thinking to myself, "This is a once in a lifetime thing, and you better make it count. You will never get to see most of these wonderful people again. Make it count."

It was an emotional, amazing day. If anybody was at all slighted or mistreated by anybody when parking, or trying to get in, or standing in line, I feel personally responsible. I'm sorry. I heard afterwards some people were mistreated. I'm so sorry.

The Heartland musicians Michael Ginsburg, Tom Jester, and Evan Carawan play as Doug directs.

A Gathering of Friends

Ray Hicks in his last days.

Bill Jones always elicits this reation from me.

By the afternoon, the temperature had soared to over one hundred degrees. It slowed us down a little, but nobody seemed to mind. Ray Ball was there, and our grabblers came. Rick Stroud, Maude—the fried pie lady from Mutton Hollow, Billie Noland, Wiley Oakley's grand-daughter—Lucinda's daughter. Ernie Profit and his family came. He carried Charlie Garland's stove. Our friends Abe and Dee Whitehead and others from our wonderful community in Happy Valley came, too.

Travis and his dad, Jerry Hughes, who built my home with his own hands and taught us how to chink a cabin and a million other things, was there. Bobby Fulcher, Tony Thomas, reenactors, artists; birder, Jim Campbell; Terry Chandler, Butler Tipton, the cavers, our Big South Fork friends, Richard Jennings, judges, sheriffs, convicts, and criminals, they were all there!

Porter High basketball players. Charlie Rhodarmer from the Sequoyah Museum, Max Ramsey, Bud Albers, Betty Best, Glenn Cardwell, and hundreds more came by that unforgettable day. There were Bohanons everywhere, and Ogles, Slavens, Terrys, Huskeys, Headricks, Richard Maples, Larry Mathis and Bud Brewster, Fiddler Danny Gammon, who for twenty-five years fiddled with us whenever we asked him. That's the way it was on *The Heartland Series*!

Bit Rouse is gone—the one-armed fiddler, and so is his brother, Jimmy, and Maynard, and the Organizer and the Moonshiner—Eulyss Roberts, and racecar drivers Breezy Wynn and Tootle Estes; Ode Reagan, Ott the Miller, the great carver; Walter Powell, John Bird Webb, the Mayor of Townsend; Effie Baker—the teller of tales. Remember "Joney and the Whale?"

Ray Hicks is gone, too, and Jep Mackey—the hoop net fisherman from Hancock County and the Toy Man, Ray Shular; Doc Barton, Fred Brown—the Holly Man; and Jesse Butcher, Jeanette Martin, Willie Sharpe, and Ethel Birchfield, Leonard Tate—the great poet of Grundy County; and the amazing Johnny Ray Hicks.

Dora Moore is gone now, too. And Thelma and Miss Pete, Arlenia West, Oma Lewis, Pat Roddy, Margaret Stevenson, Hugh Bowman, Chet Atkins, John Rice's turkey, Pauline Huff, Eddie George, Walt Martin, Stuart Maher, and Joe Diehl are all gone now. But they were there with us in spirit on this day I know, and in our thoughts.

All of us who were there celebrated their lives and all of those *Heartland* people who weren't able to be with us that day, like Jim Dykes; and the ones that could. It was both a celebration and a memorial service at the same time.

John Rice and Howard Baker, Jim Hart, Carl Williams, Bill Williams, Edye Ellis were all there.

Becky Webb and Carlock Stooksbury.

What a day! We had Linda, Laura, Amy; our wonderful editors, Amy Palmer and Ernie Ingle; Amy Anderson; Rod Kirby, our first videographer; Bill Archer, our sound man for thousands of stories; every one of our *Heartland* producers, videographers, and editors.

The original *Heartland* musicians came by and played, too: Tom Jester, Michael Ginsburg, Evan Carawan; along with Robinella, and the Boone Family, Jerry Tipton, the Harlan Kentucky Boys Choir, and so many more musicians. It seemed like everybody who ever had anything to do with the show came. It was quite a party! Then, it was over.

Down and out after a great day.

CHAPTER 18

The Epilogue

That night after "A Gathering of Friends," I remember stopping at Linda Billman's house about 9:00 on the way home. Sean Kirk, our first writer/producer, flew in from Seattle, where he lives now, to be with us. It was wonderful to see him. Linda had arranged to have a party for all of us since so many old friends were in town. Edye Ellis came by, as did many others. Dear Laura was there, too, with her husband, Robert.

We went home after it was all over and rested for a few days. Then, we got up and began our new lives without *The Heartland Series*.

Sam Moore still works at WBIR-TV, and continues taking care of all the business and promotions connected with the *Series*. He arranges the scheduling of the *Heartland* episodes and writes and produces what's needed. The *Series* continues to air on Channel 10.

Heartland videographer and co producer, Douglas D. (the "D" is for Danger) Mills is busier than ever, teaching television and camera production at Lincoln Memorial University in Harrogate, Tennessee. He continues to work and be the best freelance videographer in the South. Doug is also writing, producing, and editing television scripts. He's busy with projects for River Media, Steve Dean and his Famfive Productions, and the Princess Theater Productions in Harriman, Tennessee.

Doug and I still work together often. We talk two or three times a week. We've worked together so long; I don't think we could stop if we wanted to!

We've coproduced video projects for Sequoyah Birthplace Museum, Sevier County Bank, a Patricia Neal Commemoration for Covenant Health, "Mountain Renaissance," and the story of Pi Beta Phi Settlement School, with Laura Armour.

By himself, Doug videotaped the entire 2010 Harriman Christmas Parade that was carried live on Channel 15 Television, as its premiere production. The Government/Educational TV station is part of the new Princess Theater Educational Complex in Harriman and part of Roane State Community College.

Steve Dean continues to work on other assorted projects, including a Civil War effort, and work for the McClung Museum and Maryville College. In 2010, he rounded up part of the old *Heartland* staff, and with Julie Morris as Executive Producer, produced four, one-hour *Heartland* Productions. They continue to air on WBIR –TV, Channel 10.

So, the *Series* still has a presence on WBIR. *Heartland* Special Productions ran every three months in 2010, and included the first full-length *Heartland* one-hour drama, "Christmas Furlough." Steve also wrote and produced "A Place by the River," the story of the Ijams Family, which aired in the fall, and was nominated for an Emmy Award. And it looks like there will be more *Heartland* one-hour specials in the future.

As for me, I've been producing and writing, and have had more of a chance to act on stage. Last spring, I played Atticus Finch in Roane State Community College's production of "To Kill a Mockingbird." I also portrayed the character of Ira in "Christmas Furlough," for WBIR, Channel 10.

I've been working as a spokesperson for the economic development of Sevier County, Hallsdale/Powell Utility, and the City of Harriman, in addition to "Speechifying," as Doug calls it. I recently portrayed Einstein in "Einstein the Man," in Philadelphia for the 125th anniversary of Pi Beta Tau Engineering Fraternity, and in Crossville, Tennessee, for the Palace Theater. I'm sure there'll be more of the same in the future. So, "Don't cry for me, Argentina!" At least not yet! I'm a lucky, lucky man.

The Sequel—Another Day, Another Play

I've known for about twenty-five years, maybe longer, that I wanted to write this book. It's because I've spent so much of my life listening (talking, too), hearing, collecting, telling, and retelling stories. I've wanted, simply, to write them down and tell them over again. Finally, this is that chance. This book is the result.

It should have been out earlier. It would have, but, it took me six months to get over and understand what "A Gathering of Friends" was all about.

The shock of that event, the blast of it, ten thousand people showing up in one-hundred-degree heat to say Godspeed to the *Series,* is just staggering to me. It took a while to deal with it.

After some time off, and a little rest, like Bilbo Baggins, I'll be off again on some new adventures. What life has in store, I do not know. Already, I've lived a life beyond my wildest dreams. I look forward to what each day holds. I learned that doing *The Heartland Series*. All we can do is try to be of as much service to as many folks as possible, and to do our best.

Writing this book has allowed me to spend time with many of my old friends again, if only in my memory. For that, I am grateful. It has been a pleasure and I hope you've enjoyed it.

It has been quite a party, hasn't it?

Adieu.

Rocky Top looking down Eagle Creek.

ACKNOWLEDGMENTS

It takes many people to write a book. These are friends who helped me with mine. Some read it and made helpful comments, some provided pictures and others information. Hopefully, I've not forgotten too many of you, dear friends, who made this book possible.

Earl and Inez Adams
Steve Ahlstedt
Clopper and Joan Almon
Bill Archer
Laura Armour
Pat Ezzell Bernard
Betty Best
Linda Billman
Stretch Blanton
Tom Bosch
Linda Bosket
Glenn and Faye Cardwell
Patsy Carson
Bruce Carson
Jefferson Chapman
Em Turner Chitty
Jim Claborn
Steve Cotham
Alan Cressler
Matt Culp
Scott Danforth

Steve Dean
Kim Delozier
Dale Ditmanson
Peg Duthie
Charlie and Terry Faulkner
Will Fontanez
Bobby Fulcher
Jay Franklin
Marti Hamilton
Marvin Hammond
Jim Hart
Annette Hartigan
Leslie Hebert
Cherel Henderson
Ed Henson
Linda Ingle
Galen Johnson
Jim Johnston
Tammy Kaousias
Matt Kulp
David Luttrell

Kenneth Lynch
Sylvia Lynch
Terry Maddox
Wilma Maples
Jeff Daniel Marion
Barbara Martocci
Jim Marziotti
Dariel Mayer
Elaine Meyer
Douglas D. Mills
Nell Moore
Sam Moore
Steve Moore
Julie Morris
Lisa Myers
Judy Nelson
Billie Noland
Kathryn Pagles
Jim and Joan Phillips
James Pippen
Mike Povia

Roy Price
George A. Reeves
Charlie Rhodarmer
Margie Ribble
Dorothy Russell
Kay Sharp
Jan Simek
Peggy Maher Smith
Lorene Smith
Neil Smith
Bill Stivers
Mike Steely
Sam Tillery
Sam Venable
Harry Wade
J.V. Waller
Mrs. Judy Watson
Ryan Webb
Don Williams
Peggy Sue Woods

Beersheba Springs Historical Society
Blount County Public Library
Great Smoky Mountains Natural History Association
Great Smoky Mountains National Park Library
East Tennessee Historical Society & McClung Collection
Knoxville News-Sentinel
Medicine Man Shop
Museum of Appalachia
Sequoyah Birthplace Museum
Tennessee Valley Authority
WBIR-TV, Channel 10

CREDITS

Bartram's Gardens: drawing of snapping turtle, portrait of William Bartram • **Bill Landry Collection**: 1985 *Heartland* crew, Mann Ledbetter, Cas Walker and friends, Dolly Parton • **Blount County Library Archives:** Kathryn Pagles for W. O. Garner photographs • **Bobby Fulcher:** Rolle Holle marbles set • **Boone Family:** photo of horse people • **Charles and Terry Faulkner:** petroglyphs and Dr. Faulkner • **Dorothy Russell:** Kenneth Russell • **Douglas D. Mills:** Bohanons, *Heartland* ladies; Lucinda Oakley Ogle, Maynard and Bill, Bohanons and Bill, Linda Billman, Doug, John Rice and Bill, Bill Jones and Bill • **Faye and Glenn Cardwell:** Glenn Cardwell • **Garland Family**: Jake and Jim Garland with moonshine still • **George A. Reeves:** Map of Cherokee Villages • **Galen Johnson and Lisa Myers:** Porter High girls basketball • **Inez and Earl Adams:** Maynard Ledbetter, Ray's house, Ray Hicks • **Jan Simek:** Devilstep Hollow cave and Alabama cliff art by **Alan Creswell** • **Jay Franklin**: third unnamed cave, Landry in stupor • **Jefferson Chapman:** Tellico Archeology • **Jim Phillips:** maps of Park, Sams Creek, Mellinger Death Ridge, Tennessee Government 1796, and photo of Wilnoty • **Judy Nelson**: Dorothy Kiggans set • **Judy Watson**: Hal Watson • **Julie Morris**: Bill and Doug climbing, Julie and Doug • **Kay Sharpe**: Hayes Lossiah, Tom Underwood, William Lossiah • *Knoxville News-Sentinel*: 1992 *Heartland* staff • **Laura Armour Collection**: Lynn Leopper, Joe Cable, Jim Hart, Cris Gallu, Pelton's Bear photographs, Doug Mills, Roscoe Stinnett's field photos, Dr. Sharp and Bill, Steve Dean, Doyle Dixon, Frances Hudson, Bill Archer, Linda Billman and work crew, Opal Hatmaker, Joanne Woods and Linda Billman, Laura Armour, WBIR engineers. **Leslie Hebert**: William Hebert • **Linda Ingle**: Luther Woods and family • **Margie Ribble**: Margaret Stevenson • **Marti Hamilton**: Claborn, Landry, and Venable • **Mike Povia Collection**: for "Winter on LeConte" • **Mike Steely**: spelunkers, solo cavers, Roy Price • **Museum of Appalachia**: Elaine Meyer and Jim Marziotti for photos of Joe Deihl, Elmer Sherwood • **National Park Archives**: postcard, Mountain View Hotel, Delozier with hog, tourists, bear, Big South Fork bear move, map of Tennessee Government 1796, Native American woman, pipe and insect art by Wilnoty, Mingo Falls, Quill Rose, young Lucinda Oakley Ogle, Wiley Oakley, Wiley's shop, Henry Ford, moonshine still, CCC camp, Black Will Walker, Barry the ox, Kim Delozier, red wolf project, copperhead, peregrine falcon, otter, rhododendron • **Nell Moore**: Museum of Appalachia • **Peggy Maher Smith and Neil**: Stuart Maher • **Ryan Webb**: Bill, Steve, and Jim Hart; Bill and Joe Long; Charlie; everyone in a *Heartland* episode; boy with axe; *Heartland* musicians; Becky Webb and Carlock Stookesbury; Bill on ground; and assorted group photos from "Gathering of Friends" • **Sammy Tillery**: Walnut Bottoms, Sam Tillery on Red Bud • **Sam Moore**: "13" shoot, ghost, Sam Moore on Fontana • **Steve Ahlstedt**: Duck River • **Steve Moore**: front cover photo, back cover photo, Sams Creek, Marks Creek, clouds over mountain, mist over water, bears, trout restoration work, damaged jeep, fisheries work • **'Stretch' Blanton**: Landry, Etnier, and Venable • **TVA Archives**: Archivists Pat Ezzell Bernard and Barbara Martocci for World's Fair, flatboatin', steamboats, Knoxville 1935 Landing; Bob Kollar for his photographs of the World's Fair and Valley Adventure • **Will Fontanez**: map depicting Bartram's travels

Clopper and Joan Almon, Beersheba Springs Historical Society: for permissions to use the poem "Mountain People" from *All the Lost Octobers and Other Poems* by Leonard Tate, 1990, published by Beersheba Springs Historical Society, Dr. Benjamin H. Caldwell, Jr., editor.

INDEX

Illustrations indicated in bold.

Abrams Creek, 48, 58, 92, **100**
Adams, Earl, 136
Adams, Inez, 136
Adams, Paul, 29
Adolfson, Rob, 157–58
Ahlstedt, Steve, 48, **49**
Albers, Bud, 170
Alcoa, 138
Alum Cave Bluffs, 31, 33
Alum Cave Trail, 30–31
Anderson, Amy, 53, 162, 171
Anderson, Perrin, 162
Anderson County, 108
Andrews Bald, 92
April Fools episodes, 48–55, 66–67, 123, 152
Arant, Bill, 70–71, 75
Archer, Bill, 57, 69, **70**, 75, **78**, 87, 91, **140**, **148**, 157, 164, 171
Arch Rock, 31
Armour, Laura, 2, 8, **9**, 10, 48, **71**, 111, 162, **163**, 168, 170, 173
Armour, Robert, 173
Atkins, Chet, 170
aviators, 151–52

Bailey, Rendy, 111
Baker, Effie, 61, 104, 170
Baker, Howard, 170
Ball, Ray, 170
Ballew, Lukie, 153–55

Barton, Doc, 170
Bartram, John, 41, 42
Bartram, William, 2, 41–43, **41**, 60, **128**
bats, 87–88
batteries, 10, 30, 71, 125, 156
Bean Station, 148
Bear Creek Valley, 98
Beard Cane, 109
Bearden, 104
bears, 11–12, **11**, **14**, 15–21, **20**, 23–24, **23**, 97, 145, 149
Beaty, Tinker Dave, 163
Beersheba Springs, 135
Bell County (KY), 131
Belmont College, 31
Benton, 121
Best, Betty, 170
Big Greenbrier, 4
Big Sandy River, 145
Big South Fork, 17, 20, 170
Big South Fork River, 48, 92
Billman, Linda, 7, 38, 53, **71**, **78**, 86–89, **86**, **87**, 91, 110, **140**, **162**, 168, 170, 173
Birchfield, Ethel, 12–13, 170
birds, 8, 46, **48**, 66, 152, 159, **Plate 4**. *See also* turkeys
Birdwell, Michael, 162
Bivens, Russell, 169
Blackburn, Bill, 148

Blenheim Mine, 64, 89
Blount County, x, 134–35, 152
Blount Memorial Hospital, 21–22
blowguns, 64–66
boar, **10**, 15, 73, 123–25, **124**. *See also* hogs
boats, 69, 80–84, **81**, **82**, **83**, 87, 126, **128**. *See also* Navy; Valley Adventure
Bohanon, A.D., **3**, 5, 6, **Plate 3**
Bohanon, Walter, **3**, **4**, 3–5, 6, **Plate 3**
Bohanon family, 6, 170
Boone (NC), 12, 98
Boone Family (musicians), 171
Bosch, Tom, 32
botanists. *See* Bartram, William; Cardwell, Glenn; Ogle, Lucinda Oakley; Sharp, Aaron "Jack"
Bowman, Hugh, 170
Branstetter, Ron, 133
Brewster, Bud, 116, 170
Brewster, Willie, **115**
Brown, Fred, 138–39, **138**, 170
Brown, Herrick, 29
Bryson City, 21, 23–24
buffalo, 74–75
Bullhead, **87**
Bureau of Alcohol, Tobacco, and Firearms, 110
Burge, Miss Pete, 114, 170

[181]

Burge, "Pistol" Pete, 114
Burggraf, Don, **163**
Burrell, Elsie, 2
Butcher, Jesse, 170
Butler, Doc, 136
Buttons, Red, 121

Cable, Joe, 2, 5, 7, **8**, 108
Cades Cove, 3, 11–13, 37–39, 43, **136**, 137. *See also* Ledbetter, Maynard
Calhoun, Walker, 61
Campbell, Carlos, 95
Campbell, Jim, 170
Campbell County, 90
Campbell family, 90–91
Carawan, Evan, 7, **169**, 171
Cardwell, Faye, 96
Cardwell, Glenn, 10, 85, 96–97, **96**, 170
Carson, John, **124**
Carter High School, 117
Carver, George Washington, 138
Cas Walker Farm and Home Hour, 116
Cataloochie, 11, 21, 23, 53
catfish, 126–28, **126**, **127**
Catoosa Wildlife Management Area, 114
cavers, **90**, 158–60, 170, **Plate 11**
CCC camp, **110**
Chandler, Terry, 170
Chapman, Jefferson, 48, 57, 141, **143**
Chapman Highway, 109, 120
Charlie (grip), 70, 75
Chattanooga, ix, 9, 43, 48, 80, **81**, 83, 92
Chattanooga City High School, 134
Cherokee country, **56**, 57, 60
Cherokee Orchard Trail, 27
Cherokees, 42, 48, **56**, 57–63, 141, **142**, 151

Cherry, Travis, 131, 133
Chilhowee, 40
Chimneys, **159**, **163**
Churchill, Winston, 126–27
Citico Creek, 48, 92
Citizen Soldiers (Ambrose), 121
Clabo, Herb, 85, 112
Claborn, Jim, **55, 148**, 149, 167
Clark, Jay, 17
Clay County, 131–33
Clinch Mountain, 104
Clinch River, 48, 50–51, 80, 98, 123
Clingmans Dome, 40, 57, 72, 73, 91, 92
Clinton, 136
coal mines, 44, 64, 89–91, 108
Cocke County, 21, 107
Coker Creek, 44, 77
Coldetz Cove, 92
Collins, Russel, **132**, **133**
condoms, 126–27
contracts, 2, 7, 163, 164
Cooper, Mr. (millstone sharpener), 77–78
corporate sponsors. *See* sponsors of *Heartland*
Corryton, 104, 105
cougars. *See* panthers
Covenant Health, 173
cows, 78, 114, 115
coyotes, 151
C. P. & Walker, 86
Crockett, Davy, 123, 148, 167
Crossville, 174
crows, 57–58, 60
Cumberland and Franklin, **146–47**
Cumberland County, 114
Cumberland Falls, 92
Cumberland Mountains, 80
Cumberland Plateau, 17, 135, 157, 163. *See also* Big South Fork
Cumberland River, 102

Dale Hollow Lake, 92, 131
Dallas Theater Center, ix
Daniel Boone State Park, 64
Davis, John, 3–4, 75, 124
Dean, Steve, ix, 1, 2, 5, 7–8, **10**, 29, 47, 50–52, **50, 78**, 85, 86, 91, 108, 111, 115–16, 137, **140**, 152, 162, **164**, 165, 173–74
Deep Creek, 64
Delozier, Kim, 2, **10**, 11, 20, 23, 55, 73, 87, 123–25, **124**, 167
Delozier, Mr. (Kim's father), 54
Denton, Neal, 66
Devilstep Hollow Cave, **Plate 12**
Dewitt, Donelle, 16
Dickinson, Calvin, 162
Dictionary of Southern Mountain Speech (Montgomery), 101
Diehl, Joe, 44, **45**, 170
Dinner Bell Restaurant, 154
Dixon, Doyle, **50**, 51
Dorsey, "Pot," 107
Doyle High School, 117
Duck River, **49**
Dungannon (VA), 71, 80, 83–84
Dyer, Bobby, 133
Dykes, Jim, 170

Eagle Creek, 87
eastern cougar. *See* panthers
East Tennessee History Center, 59, 102
East Tennessee State University Appalachian Folklore Department, 98
Efler, Larry, 169
"Einstein the Man," ix, 174
Elizabethton, 12
elk, 11, 53, 54, 73
Elkmont, 3, 73, 112
Eller, Kiley, 111
Ellis, Edye, 170, 173
Elsa, 98

episodes
- "Bartram's Trail," 42
- "Bats on the Wing," 87
- "Bushwackers," 163
- "Cades Cove—The Homeplace," 37
- "Catching Snapping Turtles," 128–29, 151
- "Cherokee Dawn," 151
- "Cherokee Zenith," 151
- "Christmas Furlough," 174
- "Climbing LeConte," 29, 151
- "A Cold Day," 151
- "Coon Hunting," 155
- "The Cow Barn," 12, 13, 85, 93–94
- "The Discovery," 162
- "Downstream: From the Mountains to the Ocean," 71–73
- "Electric Trees," 52–53
- "European Wild Boar," 125
- "Family Mine," 90–91
- "Fishin'," 2–5
- "Flatboatin'," 80–84
- "The Flint Mine," 156–60
- "The Fly Boys," 151–52
- "A Gift for Jacob," 9
- "Grabblin'," 126–28, 151
- "Gritted Bread," 64
- "Haints," 111
- "The Holly Man," 138–39
- "The Homecoming," 37, 137
- "The Homeplace," 12, 13
- "LeConte Lodge," 29, 151
- "The Legend of Jonathan Swift's Lost Silver Mine," 141
- "Lucinda," 2
- "The Memoirs and Journey of Lt. Henry Timberlake," 141
- "The Moonshiner," 107–9
- "The Move," 152
- "Opossum and Sweet Potatoes," 102–5, 153
- "Our Native Tongue," 98
- "Paradise Recaptured," 8
- "A Peck to the Hill," 99
- "A Place by the River," 174
- "The Sharpshooter," 149
- "The Sheep Eye," 94
- "A Significant Find," 50–52
- "Tanning a Hide," 155
- "13," **114**
- "The Trail of Tears," 60
- "Treasure Hunters," 143, 151
- "Wake and Funeral of Jim Claborn," **55**
- "Watermelon Slippin'," 152
- "The Watt Experiment," 52–53
- "We Endure—The Journey of the Cherokee," 57
- "Wiley's Dog Gone," 94
- "William Bartram—The Flower Hunter," 2, 7, 41, 93
- "Winter on LeConte," 151
- "Working in Coal," 89–90

Estes, Tootle, 170
Etnier, David, 48, **52**
Everett High School, 135

Famfive Productions, 173
Farmer, Gary, 66
Faulkner, Charles, 47, **48**, 51, 156
Ferguson, Champ, 163
First Families of Tennessee Project, 59
First Tennessee Bank, 152
fish, 5, 48, 71–72, 152 (*see also* catfish; trout)
fishing, **2**, 3–5, **3**, **4**, **52**, 60–61, 126–28, 170, **Plate 3**
flatboats, 80–84, **83**
flint, 64, 156–59
Floyd, Buddy, 54
Flynn's Lick, 44
Ford, Henry, **95**
Ford cars, 23, 24
Fontana Lake, 87, **162**

Fontana Village Marina, 87
Fort Oglethorpe (GA), 119
Fort Pitt, 145, 149
Fothergill, Dr. (friend of William Bartram), 42
Fox, Eric, 169
Foxfire books, 152
Francis, Gil, 54
Francis, Steve [pseud.], 21–23
Franklin, map of, **146–47**
French Broad River, 80, 92
fried pie, 9, 170
Frome, Michael, 42
Frost, Robert, 138
Fulcher, Bobby, **130**, 131–32, 170

Gallu, Cris, **12**, 12–13
Gammon, Danny, 170
Gannett Corporation, 163–64
Garner, W. O., photographs by, **100, 101**
Garland, Charlie, stove of, 109, 170
Garland, Jake, **109**
Garland, Jim, **109**
Garver, Lenny, 21–22, 23–24
Gate City (VA), 79
Gatlinburg, 5–6, **6**, 10, 32, 40, 93, 94, 112, 125
Gatlinburg Garden Club, 85
George, Eddie (fisherman), 170
Gheen, Tom, 153–54
Ginsburg, Michael, 7, **169**, 171
goats, **54**
Gowey, David, 75–76
grabblers, 126–28, 170
Grainger County, 104
Graves, Clay, 104, 105
Great Buzzard, 58
Great Smoky Mountains National Park, founding of, 1, 8, 93, 95
Greenbrier, 2–3, 96
Gregory's Bald, 92

groundhogs, 153–54
Grundy County, 135, 170

Hall, Ronnie, **163**
Hallsdale/Powell Utility, 174
Hamblin County, 111
Hancock County, 170
Happy Hiker, 32–33, **32**, **33**
Happy Valley, 58, 66, 104, 170
Harlan Kentucky Boys Choir, 171
Harper, Jack, 2
Harriman, 152, 173, 174
Harrogate, 173
Hart, Jim, 1, 6, 7, **10**, 47, **78**, **164**, 170
Hatmaker, Opal, 136, **137**
Headrick family, 170
Hebert, Leslie, 66
Hebert, William (Two Bears), **66**, 66–67
Hendrix, John, 98
Henry, Gary, **125**
Henson, Michael Paul, 143–44
Hercules Club, 40–41
Hiawasee River, 64, 80
Hicks, Benjamin, 98
Hicks, Johnny Ray, 102, 123, 170
Hicks, Ray, 14, 97, 98–102, **99**, **170**
Hicks, Rosie, 98
Highway 33, 119
Highway 129 ("the dragon"), 87, 88
Highway 441, 57, 125
hogs, **10**, 11, 73, 79, 123–25, **124**
Holder, Mr. (watermelon grower), 153
Holder, Jennifer, 153
Holder, Jesse, 77
holly, 138–39
Holston River, 80, 92
Hoop Creek, 151
horses, **22**, 25–30, **26**, **27**, 143, 148, 151, 166, 167

Howard Johnson's, 125
Hudson, Frances, **54**
Huff, Jack, **30**
Huff, Pauline, 170
Hughes, Jerry, 170
Hughes, Travis, 170
Hunt, Carson, 169
Huskey, Oliver, 97
Huskey family, 170

Ice Water Springs, 124–25
Ijams family, 174
Indian Wars, **145**, 149
Ingle, Ernie, 8, 149
Irwin, John Rice, 44, 50, **70**, **164**, 165, 170. *See also* Museum of Appalachia
Ison, Margie, ix

jaguars, 15, 48
Jarmalo, Ken, 2, 6
Jeffries Hell, **124**
Jellico, 143, 149
jellyfish, 162
Jennings, Richard, 170
Jester, Tom, 7, **169**, 171
Johnson, Galen, 134–35
Jones, Bill, 167, **170**
Jones, Hal, 152
Junaluska, Marie, 57–59
Junior (marble player), 131, 132

Kenwell, 43
Kephart, Horace, 88
Kerns Bakery, 120
Kiggans, Dorothy, 117–18, **118**
Kill Devil Hills (NC), 92
Kingston, 77, 80
Kingston Pike, 78
Kirby, Rod, ix, 2, 4, 91, 171
Kirk, Sean, 2, 7, 8–9, **9**, 10, 11, 48, 98, 109, 124, 173
Kirkland Falls, 2
Kitts (KY), 89

Knoxville, x, 1, 33, 44, 54, 57, **80**, 86, 102, 108, 117, 119–20, 128, 152, 153–54
Knoxville Journal, 120
Knoxville Utilities Board, 44
Kuralt, Charles, 98

La Fete, 92
Landry, Becky, ix–x, 40–41, 104–5, 154
Landry, Jack, x, **39**, 149, 153
Landry family members, x, 9, 14, 23, 152. *See also* Landry, Becky; Landry, Jack
Lanier High School, 135
Leach, Cathy, 7
LeConte, 25–36, **26**, **28**, **30**, **31**, **36**, 43, 71, 92, 151, 156
LeConte Lodge, 26, 28–29, **30**, 34, **35–36**
Ledbetter, Mann, **38**
Ledbetter, Maynard, 12, 37–39, **39**, 107, 137, 170
Lee, Jeff, 165
Lenoir City, 117–18, 154
Leopper, Lynn, 7, **8**
Lewis, Lee, 32
Lewis, Oma, 123, 170
Lincoln Memorial University, 173
Line, Tim, 29, 31, 34
Little Greenbrier Schoolhouse, 2
Little People, 61–62
Little River, 3, 5, 73, 92, **Plates 2–3**, **Plate 8**
Little Tennessee River Valley, 60, **142**
llamas, 26
Lone Mountain, 151
Long, Joe, **165**, 167
The Longest Day, 121
Look Rock, 40
Lossiah, Hayes, **59**, 61, 64–66, **65**
Lossiah, William, 61, 64, 66, **67**, **68**
Loudon County, 118, 155

Lowe's, 128
Lucinda (Oakley Ogle), 2, 6, 84–85, **84**, **85**, 93, 95, 170

Mackey, Jep, 170
Maggie B (boat), **103**
Magnotti, Alexis, 8, **71**, **154**, 155
Maher, Stuart, 2, 43–44, **43**, 170
Mankiller, Johnny, 59
Manteo (NC), 92
Maples, Richard, 170
Marble Kings, 131
marbles, 131–33, **132**, **133**
Market Street Bridge, **81**
Martin, Jeanette, 13, 170
Martin, Walt, 170
Maryville, 21, 43, 109, 121
Maryville College, 173
Maryville jail, **109**
Mathis, Larry, 114, 116, 170
Mathis, Thelma, 114–15, 116, 170
Maude (fried pie lady), 170
Mayer, Elaine, 165
Maynardville Highway, 120
McCarroll, Charlie, **130**
McClerren Marble Yard, **132**
McClung Museum, 48, 57, 141, **143**, 173
McWhirter, Ken, 7
Medicine Man Shop, 58, 60–61, 68
Mellinger, Jasper, 93, 111–13
Mellinger family, 112, 113
Mellinger Death Ridge, 112, **113**
Memphis, 102
Memphis Melrose High School, 134
Miller, Bob, 53
Mills, Douglas "Danger," 2, 3, 4, 7, **9**, 10, 11–12, 15–20, **16–17**, **21**, 22, 25, 27, 28, 29–30, **29**, 31, 33–34, **34**, **38**, 48, 54, 57, 58, 62, 63, 64, 69, 71, 73, 74, 77, **78**, 83, 86, **87**, **88**, 89–90, **89**, 91–92, **91**, 97, 98, **111**, **114**, 121, 124–25, 126, 128, 129, **140**, 143, 149, **153**, 154, 156, **158**, **159**, 160, 161, 162, **163**, **164**, 165, 166, 168, **169**, 173, 174, **Plate 7**
Mingo Falls, 63–64, **63**
Mississippi River, 102
Monday, George, 145, 148–50
monkeys, 75–76
Monroe County, 128, 153
Montgomery, Michael, 100–101
Mooney, James, 58, 63–64, 67, 68
moonshine, **106**, 107–11, **109**, 136
Moore, Dora, 170
Moore, Sam, **111**, 161, **162**, 173
Moore, Steve, 71–72, **73**, 167
Morgan County, 55, 108, 109–10, 114
Morris, Julie, 162, **163**, 165, 166, 168, 169, 173
Morristown, 148
Morton's Overlook, 40
Moses, George, 126–29
mountain lions. *See* panthers
"Mountain People" (Tate), 135–36
Mountain View Hotel, 5–6, **6**
Mt. LeConte. *See* LeConte
Mt. Mitchell, 92
Mt. Sterling, 21, 23
The Mule Man (Joe Long), **165**, 167
mules, **155**
Murphy (NC), 64, 67
Museum of Appalachia, 6, 44, **45**, **92**, 165, 168. *See also* Irwin, John Rice
music for the series, 7, 8, 69
mussels, 48, **49**, 152
Mussel Shoals (AL), 116
Mutton Hollow, 170
Myers, Selma, 39
Myths and Legends of the Cherokee (Mooney), 58, 63–64, 67, 68

Nantahala River, 92
Native Americans, 42, 57–68, **58**, **59**, **65**, **66**, **67**, **68**, 73–75, 141, 143, 148, 149, 151, 156–59, 162
Nature Conservancy, 73
Navy, 117, 118
Newfound Gap, 40, 57–58, 123–25
New Orleans (LA), 80, 92
Ninety-Nines, 151
Noland, Billie, 170
Norris Dam, 52
Norris Lake, 92, 119
Notre Dame High School, ix

Oakdale, 114
Oakley, Wiley, 12, 13, 84, 85, 93–96, **94**, **95**, 112, 170
Oak Ridge, 2, **9**, 98
Obed River Gorge, 55, 71
Ocoee River, 92
Oconaluftee River, 57, 60, 62, 64, 65
Oconaluftee Village, 57, **59**, 151
Ogle, Charlie, 112
Ogle, Lucinda Oakley, 2, 6, 84–85, **84**, **85**, 93, 95, 170
Ogle family, 170
Ogle's Store, 112
O'Keeffe, Georgia, 74
Oliver Springs, 107
opossums, 102–5, 153
Osgood, Charles, 98
Ott the Miller, 170
Ownby, Lem, 112
oxen, 137, **139**

Palmer, Amy, 8, **140**, 149, 171
Panhandle Pete [James Howard Nash, pseud.], **115**
panthers, 55, 78, 87–88, 97, 101
Parmalee, Paul, 48, 71
Parsons Branch Road, 20
Parton, Dolly, 116, **Plate 10**
Patterson, Gene, 126

Patton, George, 121–22
Peale, Charles Wilson, **41**
Pellissippi State Community College, ix
Pelton, Mike, 15, **16**, 17
petroglyphs, 47, **48**, 156, **159**, **160**, **Plate 12**
Pi Beta Phi Settlement School, 85, 173
Pittman Center, 96
planting by signs, 78, 151
Poor Valley, 104
Porter, Victor, **111**
Porter High School, 134–35, **134**, 170
Powell, Walter, 170
Powell River, 80
Povia, Mike, 32
Price, Roy, 143, **144**
Princess Theater, 116, 173
Profit, Ernie, 170
Prometheus (cave), 158–60
Puncheon Camp, 104
Pyatt, Joe, 98

Qualla Boundary, 57, 60
quilters, 6, 136, **137**
quilts, 37

raccoons, 155
Raccoon Valley, 78
rafts, 25, 80–84, **82**, **83**
Rainbow Falls, **28**
Ramsey, Andy, 30–31, 75
Ramsey, Max, 170
Reagan, Ode, 170
Red (revenuer), 136
red wolves, 11, 15, 123, **125**, **Plate 5**
Reelfoot Lake, 92, 123
Reeves, Bradley, 102
Reeves, George A., 56
Rennie, 77

Rhodarmer, Charlie, 170
Rhoton, Wayne, 133
rifles. *See* guns
River Media, 173
Roane County, ix, 108
Roane Mountain, 12, 92
Roane State Community College, 116, 173, 174
Roaring Fork Creek, 111–12
Roberts, Eulyss, 107–9, 170
Robertsville, 98
Robinella, 171
Rockwood, **88**
Rocky Top, 92
Roddy, Pat, 170
Rogers, Doris, 135
Rogers, Marie, 135
rolle holle, 131–33
Roosevelt, Eleanor, 95
Roosevelt, Franklin, 95
Rose, Aunt Barth, 114–15
Rose, Bill, 114
Rose, Dit, 114
Rose, Jim, 114
Rose, Joe, 114
Rose, Quill, 79
Rouse, Bit, 170
Rouse, Jimmy, 170
Russell, Ken, 120–22, **121**, **122**

SAMAB, 72–73
Sams Creek, 72, **74**
Scarboro, 98
Sequoyah, 123
Sequoyah Birthplace Museum, 170, 173
Sevier, John, 123
Sevier County, 26, 109, 174
Sevier County Bank, 173
Sevierville, 40, 57, 112
Seymour Elementary School, 53–55
Shape Note Singers, 6

Sharp, Aaron "Jack," 6, 39–41, **39**, **40**, 42, 84, 123
Sharpe, Willie, 170
Sharps Chapel, 119–20, **120**
Shaw (grip), 73–75
Sherwood, Elmer, **92**
Shular, Ray, 170
Simek, Jan, 48, 156–59, **157**, **158**, 170
Slaven family, 170
snakes, 62, 64, 91, 114, 128, 158, 159, **Plate 6**
snapping turtles, 128–29, **128**, **129**
soapstone, 62–63, 64, 67–68
Smoky Mountain Wildflower Pilgrimage, 39, 85
Southern Appalachian Man and the Biosphere (SAMAB), 72–73
Southern Highlanders (Kephart), 88
Southern Mountain Speech (Williams), 100–101
spelunkers, **90**, 158–60, 170, **Plate 11**
Spence Field, 92
sponsors of *Heartland*, 2, 5–6, 7, 12–13, 72–73
State Technical Institute, ix
Steely, Mike, 143, **144**, **149**
Stevenson, Margaret, 30–31, **31**, 170
Stinnett, Roscoe, **29**, **88**, **152**, **153**
Stivers, Bill, 87
Stooksbury, Carlock, 171
Strangers in High Places (Frome), 42
Stroud, Rick, 148, 149, 170
Sugarlands, 96, **110**, 125
Sugarloaf Mountain, 109
Sully family, 112–13
Summitt, Pat, 135
Sutherland Avenue airport, 152
Sweetwater, 91

Sweetwater Creek, 129
Swift, Jonathan (sea merchant), 141–50
Swimmer (Cherokee Myth Keeper), 67
Swimmer, Amanda, 61

Tadlock, Sevier, 98
Tate, Leonard, 135–36, 170
Tazewell, 114, 151
Tellico archeology, 48, **51**
Tellico Plains, 44, 121
Tellico River, 48, 92
Tennessee Archive of Motion Image and Sound (TAMIS), 102
Tennessee Technological University, 162–63
Tennessee River, ix, 71, 80, 103, 126
Tennessee Valley Authority (TVA), ix, **x**, **51**, 52, 53, 54, 73, 80, 102
Terry family, 170
Thomas, Farris, 151–52
Thomas, Ruth, 151
Thomas, Tony, **130**, 170
Thompson, Jim, 95
Thompson, Stephanie Johnson, 135
Thunderhead, 92
tigers, 48
Tillery, Sam, **166**, 167
Timberlake, Henry, 141, 142
Tinsley, Jack, 131, 133
Tinsley Green, England, 131–33, **133**
Tipton, Butler, 170
Tipton, Jerry, 171
Todd, Don, 55

tourists, 10–12, **11**, 50, 94
Townsend, 3, 37, 40, 170
Townsend, Carmen, 109
Townsend High School, 135
Tremont, 3, 11, 17, 20
Trillium Gap Trail, 27, **28**, 29
trout, 2–5, 60, 71–72, **72**, 92, 152
Trout Unlimited, 73
Tuckaleechee Cove, 43
turkeys, 44, 79, 159, 170
turtles, 128–29, **128**, **129**
Tuskegee Airmen, 138
TVA. *See* Tennessee Valley Authority
Two Bears (William Hebert), **66**, 66–67
TWRA, 73

Uktana, 64
Underwood, Tom, 59, 60–61, **61**, 62, 63, 64, 67
Union Carbide, 2, 6
Union County, 119
Upper Cumberland Plateau, 163

Valley Adventure, ix, 80, 102, **103**
Varner, Rick, 73, 87
Venable, Sam, **52**, **55**
veterinarians, 136

Wade, Harry, 152
Walker, Black Will, **110**, **139**
Walker, Cas, **115**, 116
Walnut Bottoms, **26**
Wartburg, 105
Washburn, 104
watermelon patches, 152, 153
water witching, 78, 151

Watson, Hal, **22**, 26–27, **27**, 109, 111
Watts Bar Lake, 92, 126
WDVX, 86
Webb, Becky, **171**
Webb, John Bird, 170
Welsh, Harold, 32
West, Arlenia, 170
West Valley School, 153
Wheat, 98
Whidby, Jim, **144**
Whitehead, Abe, 104, 170
Whitehead, Dee, 170
Whitehead, Grady, 104
wild boar. *See* hogs
Wildflower Pilgrimage, 39, 85
Wildwood Community, 134
Wiley Shop, **94**
Williams, Bill, 170
Williams, Carl, 170
Williams, Gratis, 100–101
Wilnoty, John Julius, 61, **62**, 62–63
Windrock Mountain, 107
Wise County Community College, 80
Witcher, Mike, 169
witches, 67–68, 114–16
Wolf, Joan, 104, 105, 167
Wolfenbarger, Varnell, **163**
wolves, 11, 15, 55, **125**, **Plate 5**
World's Fair, ix, **x**, 1, 80
Wood, Elmer, 152
Woods, Joanne, 75, **162**
Woods, Luther ("Lon"), 119–20, **119**, **120**
Woodson, Kathy, 169
WRJZ, 86
Wynn, Breezy, 170

About Celtic Cat Publishing

Celtic Cat Publishing was founded in 1995 to publish emerging and established writers. The following works are available from Celtic Cat Publishing at *www.celticcatpublishing.com*, Amazon.com, and major bookstores.

Poetry
Exile: Poems of an Irish Immigrant, James B. Johnston
Marginal Notes, Frank Jamison
Rough Ascension and Other Poems of Science, Arthur J. Stewart
Bushido: The Virtues of Rei and Makoto, Arthur J. Stewart
Circle, Turtle, Ashes, Arthur J. Stewart
Ebbing & Flowing Springs: New and Selected Poems and Prose (1976-2001), Jeff Daniel Marion
Gathering Stones, KB Ballentine
Fragments of Light, KB Ballentine
Guardians, Laura Still

Humor
My Barbie Was an Amputee, Angie Vicars
Life Among the Lilliputians, Judy Lockhart DiGregorio
Memories of a Loose Woman, Judy Lockhart DiGregorio

Chanukah
One for Each Night: Chanukah Tales and Recipes, Marilyn Kallet

Children
Jack the Healing Cat (English), Marilyn Kallet
Jacques le chat guérisseur (French), Marilyn Kallet

End of Life
Being Alive, Raymond Johnston